Henry Stol

IN THE END GOD

RELIGIOUS PERSPECTIVES · VOLUME TWENTY

IN THE END GOD

JOHN A. T. ROBINSON
Bishop of Woolwich

1817

HARPER & ROW, PUBLISHERS

NEW YORK EVANSTON AND LONDON

The author and publishers wish to acknowledge their indebtedness for permission to use copyright material contained in this volume as follows: From *Report to Greco* by Nikos Kazantzakis published by Bruno Cassirer (Publishers) Ltd.; from *Some Modern Substitutes for Christianity* by Dom Bede Frost published by A. R. Mowbray & Co. Ltd.; from *The Shaking of the Foundations* by Paul Tillich published by SCM Press Ltd.; from Professor H. H. Price's article 'Psychological Research and Human Personality' which appeared in *The Hibbert Journal,* January, 1949.

FIRST EDITION

LIBRARY OF CONGRESS CATALOG CARD NUMBER: 68-17582

Contents

Religious Perspectives

VOLUMES ALREADY PUBLISHED

RELIGIOUS PERSPECTIVES

Its Meaning and Purpose

RELIGIOUS PERSPECTIVES represents a quest for the rediscovery of man. It constitutes an effort to define man's search for the essence of being in order that he may have a knowledge of goals. It is an endeavor to show that there is no possibility of achieving an understanding of man's total nature on the basis of phenomena known by the analytical method alone. It hopes to point to the false antinomy between revelation and reason, faith and knowledge, grace and nature, courage and anxiety. Mathematics, physics, philosophy, biology, and religion, in spite of their almost complete independence, have begun to sense their interrelatedness and to become aware of that mode of cognition which teaches that "the light is not without but within me, and I myself am the light."

Modern man is threatened by a world created by himself. He is faced with the conversion of mind to naturalism, a dogmatic secularism and an opposition to a belief in the transcendent. He begins to see, however, that the universe is given not as one existing and one perceived but as the unity of subject and object; that the barrier between them cannot be said to have been dissolved as the result of recent experience in the physical sciences, since this barrier has never existed. Confronted with the question of meaning, he is summoned to rediscover and scrutinize the immutable and the permanent which constitute the dynamic, unifying aspect of life as well as the principle of differentiation; to reconcile identity and diversity, immutability and unrest. He begins to recognize that just as every person descends by his particular path, so he is able to ascend, and this ascent aims at a return to the source of creation, an inward home from which he has become estranged.

It is the hope of RELIGIOUS PERSPECTIVES that the rediscovery of man will point the way to the rediscovery of God. To this end a

viii

rediscovery of first principles should constitute part of the quest. These principles, not to be superseded by new discoveries, are not those of historical worlds that come to be and perish. They are to be sought in the heart and spirit of man, and no interpretation of a merely historical or scientific universe can guide the search. RELIGIOUS PERSPECTIVES attempts not only to ask dispassionately what the nature of God is, but also to restore to human life at least the hypothesis of God and the symbols that relate to him. It endeavors to show that man is faced with the metaphysical question of the truth of religion while he encounters the empirical question of its effects on the life of humanity and its meaning for society. Religion is here distinguished from theology and its doctrinal forms and is intended to denote the feelings, aspirations, and acts of men, as they relate to total reality. For we are all in search of reality, of a reality which is there whether we know it or not; and the search is of our own making but reality is not.

RELIGIOUS PERSPECTIVES is nourished by the spiritual and intellectual energy of world thought, by those religious and ethical leaders who are not merely spectators but scholars deeply involved in the critical problems common to all religions. These thinkers recognize that human morality and human ideals thrive only when set in a context of a transcendent attitude toward religion and that by pointing to the ground of identity and the common nature of being in the religious experience of man, the essential nature of religion may be defined. Thus, they are committed to reevaluate the meaning of everlastingness, an experience which has been lost and which is the content of that *visio Dei* constituting the structure of all religions. It is the many absorbed everlastingly into the ultimate unity, a unity subsuming what Whitehead calls the fluency of God and the everlastingness of passing experience.

These volumes seek to show that the unity of which we speak consists in a certitude emanating from the nature of man who seeks God and the nature of God who seeks man. Such certitude bathes in an intuitive act of cognition, participating in the divine essence and is related to the natural spirituality of intelligence. This is not by any means to say that there is an equivalence of all

faiths in the traditional religions of human history. It is, however,
to emphasize the distinction between the spiritual and the temporal which all religions acknowledge. For duration of thought
is composed of instants superior to time, and is an intuition of
the permanence of existence and its metahistorical reality. In
fact, the symbol[1] itself found on cover and jacket of each volume
of RELIGIOUS PERSPECTIVES is the visible sign or representation of
the essence, immediacy, and timelessness of religious experience;
the one immutable center, which may be analogically related to
Being in pure act, moving with centrifugal and ecumenical necessity outward into the manifold modes, yet simultaneously, with
dynamic centripetal power and with full intentional energy, returning to the source. Through the very diversity of its authors,
the Series shows that the basic and poignant concern of every
faith is to point to, and overcome the crisis in our apocalyptic
epoch—the crisis of man's separation from man and of man's
separation from God—the failure of love. The authors endeavor,
moreover, to illustrate the truth that the human heart is able, and
even yearns, to go to the very lengths of God; that the darkness
and cold, the frozen spiritual misery of recent times, are breaking,
cracking, and beginning to move, yielding to efforts to overcome
spiritual muteness and moral paralysis. In this way, it is hoped,
the immediacy of pain and sorrow, the primacy of tragedy and
suffering in human life, may be transmuted into a spiritual and
moral triumph. For the uniqueness of man lies in his capacity for
self-transcendence.

RELIGIOUS PERSPECTIVES is therefore an effort to explore the
meaning of God, an exploration which constitutes an aspect of
man's intrinsic nature, part of his ontological substance. This
Series grows out of an abiding concern that in spite of the release
of man's creative energy which science has in part accomplished,
this very science has overturned the essential order of nature.
Shrewd as man's calculations have become concerning his means,
his choice of ends which was formerly correlated with belief in
God, with absolute criteria of conduct, has become witless. God
is not to be treated as an exception to metaphysical principles,

[1] From the original design by Leo Katz.

invoked to prevent their collapse. He is rather their chief exemplification, the source of all potentiality. The personal reality of freedom and providence, of will and conscience, may demonstrate that "he who knows" commands a depth of consciousness inaccessible to the profane man, and is capable of that transfiguration which prevents the twisting of all good to ignominy. This religious content of experience is not within the province of science to bestow; it corrects the error of treating the scientific account as if it were itself metaphysical or religious; it challenges the tendency to make a religion of science—or a science of religion—a dogmatic act which destroys the moral dynamic of man. Indeed, many men of science are confronted with unexpected implications of their own thought and are beginning to accept, for instance, the trans-spatial and trans-temporal dimension in the nature of reality.

RELIGIOUS PERSPECTIVES attempts to show the fallacy of the apparent irrelevance of God in history. This Series submits that no convincing image of man can arise, in spite of the many ways in which human thought has tried to reach it, without a philosophy of human nature and human freedom which does not exclude God. This image of *Homo cum Deo* implies the highest conceivable freedom, the freedom to step into the very fabric of the universe, a new formula for man's collaboration with the creative process and the only one which is able to protect man from the terror of existence. This image implies further that the mind and conscience are capable of making genuine discriminations and thereby may reconcile the serious tensions between the secular and religious, the profane and sacred. The idea of the sacred lies in what it *is,* timeless existence. By emphasizing timeless existence against reason as a reality, we are liberated, in our communion with the eternal, from the otherwise unbreakable rule of "before and after." Then we are able to admit that all forms, all symbols in religions, by their negation of error and their affirmation of the actuality of truth, make it possible to experience that *knowing* which is above knowledge, and that dynamic passage of the universe to unending unity.

God is here interpreted not as a heteronomous being issuing commandments but as the *Tatt-Twam-Asi:* "Do unto others as

you would have others do unto you. For I am the Lord." This
does not mean a commandment from on high but rather a self-
realization through "the other"; since the isolated individual is
unthinkable and meaningless. Man becomes man by recognizing
his true nature as a creature capable of will and decision. For
then the divine and the sacred become manifest. And though he
believes in choices, he is no Utopian expecting the "coming of
the kingdom." Man, individually and collectively, is losing the
chains which have bound him to the inexorable demands of
nature. The constraints are diminshing and an infinity of choices
becomes available to him. Thus man himself, from the sources
of his ontological being, at last must decide what is the *bonum
et malum.* And though the anonymous forces which in the past
have set the constraints do indeed threaten him with total anarchy
and with perhaps a worse tyranny than he experienced in past
history, he nevertheless begins to see that preceding the moral
issue is the cognitive problem: the perception of those conditions
for life which permit mankind to fulfill itself and to accept the
truth that beyond scientific, discursive knowledge there is non-
discursive, intuitive awareness. And, I suggest, this is not to
secularize God but rather to gather him into the heart of the
nature of matter and indeed of life itself.

The volumes in this Series seek to challenge the crisis which
separates, to make reasonable a religion that binds, and to present
the numinous reality within the experience of man. Insofar as the
Series succeeds in this quest, it will direct mankind toward a
reality that is eternal and away from a preoccupation with that
which is illusory and ephemeral.

For man is now confronted with his burden and his greatness:
"He calleth to me, Watchman, what of the night? Watchman,
what of the night?"[2] Perhaps the anguish in the human soul may
be assuaged by the answer, by the *assimilation* of the person in
God: "The morning cometh, and also the night: if ye will inquire,
inquire ye: return, come."[3]

RUTH NANDA ANSHEN

[2] Isaiah 21:11.
[3] Isaiah 21:12.

CHAPTER I

The End of God

Let me begin by saying how this book came to its present form. In 1950 there appeared in a series 'Theology for Modern Men' a book called *In the End, God ...: A Study of the Christian Doctrine of the Last Things*. It was my first publication. Indeed there was material in it (Chapters X and XI of the present book) which represented my earliest essay into the field of theology and must first have been penned in 1942 or 1943. The book was by an unknown author and published by James Clarke. The series in which it appeared expired soon afterwards. Though the book was kindly received and went into a second impression, it never broke through the limited circle to which this sort of writing was at that time confined. Those were the days before the circulation-explosion in theology—which must surely be accounted one of the more interesting phenomena of the post-religious age in which we are said to live.

When, therefore, I was asked to let it appear in a new form in a much broader context, I was happy to agree. I wondered, as I read it after an interval in which so much water had passed under the bridge, how much of it I could make my own to-day. I was surprised. In one sense, I could never write it now. In another I found I wanted to alter remarkably little. I did not wish to withdraw anything of substance I had said. Yet I could not begin to say it like that now. It was clear therefore that I must either leave it essentially as it was, with a new and extended preface, or recast it as an entirely fresh book. I had neither the inclination nor the time for the latter. So I agreed with the publishers on the form—and turned to other more urgent commitments. A book, after all, on the Last Things could surely bide its time. Nothing short of the end of the world was likely to make it out of date.

But then, in the midst of other preparations, I received urgent letters from my American editor and publisher. Would I bring forward my date-line, change the title of the book, and let it come as my contribution—and indeed my ' answer ' —to the currently raging controversy on ' the death of God '? My immediate response was to dismiss this as a gimmick. My material was written for an entirely different situation and to meet a very different set of questions. I had seen too much of this ' cashing in ' after *Honest to God* and had no desire to start doing it myself.

Then I began to ponder whether there might not after all be a real connection; and I am genuinely grateful for being made to see a link that for me at least has proved creative.

I still do not propose in this setting to enter ' the death of God controversy.' An admirably lucid assessment of it has recently appeared under this very title,[1] and with its sympathetic but discriminating conclusions I would very largely agree.[2] Suffice it to say that I suspect that *in this form* it is an eruption which will work itself out. What it has thrown up[3] does not seem to me as yet stable or solid enough to take shape in enduring structures on which others can build. (In this I should judge it is different from the closely related ferment on ' secular Christianity.'[4]) But the concerns and protests that underlie it are, I am sure, of lasting significance. They correspond—as the reverberations they have set up testify—to questions to which none of us can be insensitive. Talk of ' God ' will never be quite the

[1] Thomas W. Ogletree, *The 'Death of God' Controversy.*

[2] See further Chapter II of my book, *Exploration into God.*

[3] E.g., Thomas J. J. Altizer, *The Gospel of Christian Atheism,* and with William Hamilton, *Radical Theology and the Death of God.* The latter has a useful bibliography of the rest of the literature to date.

[4] For a popular introduction to this, see Colin Williams, *Faith in a Secular Age.* The most creative contribution is undoubtedly Harvey Cox, *The Secular City,* to whose bibliography should now be added Ronald Gregor Smith, *Secular Christianity,* and *The Secular City Debate* (ed. D. Callahan).

same again. We cannot revert to using the word or speaking about the reality in the same uncomplicated way.

The controversy in its varied, and often mixed-up, aspects revolves around two main issues: (a) whether the *word* 'God' is dead, in the sense that, either temporarily or permanently, it is now (perhaps like 'the Devil' or 'the soul') a term whose meaning-world is so limited or whose reference and cash-value are so uncertain that it has virtually ceased to be able to 'function' in contemporary society; and (b) whether the *reality* 'God' is dead, in the sense that, either temporarily or permanently, the whole dimension of 'transcendence' is lost to modern man, so that the old values—and the old Gospel—must now be re-expressed, if indeed that is possible, without reference to it.

I am not personally convinced that God is 'dead' in either sense. In fact, I am profoundly persuaded that, especially in the latter sense, he is not. But I take the questions with real seriousness. Indeed, I believe that the question left by Dietrich Bonhoeffer[5] before he was hanged by the Nazis in 1945 is perhaps the most searching question of our age: 'How do we speak in a " secular " way about " God "?'

What I want to do here, however, is to suggest that the 'answer,' if that is the right word, is perhaps as likely to be found in the area of eschatology, that is, the area of Christian faith which relates to its hope for the End, as anywhere else. That will doubtless sound paradoxical or plain nonsense. If the word 'God' is dead wood, then surely 'eschatology' is even deader. If the reality of God lies on the fading edges of human consciousness in the twentieth century, 'the Last Things' are clearly beyond the fringe.

I believe, however, that there is a genuine connection between 'the end of God' in both senses of that phrase, and that this is no mere verbal trick. In fact it is the same connection that St. Paul makes when he says in Rom. 10.4 that 'Christ is the end (or *telos*) of the law.' In Christ

[5] *Letters and Papers from Prison*, 3rd rev. ed., p. 153. (U.S.A. *Prisoner for God*.)

the Law is finished : it is also fulfilled. Similarly, St. James, in a passage that I make the heading of a subsequent chapter, says : 'You . . . have seen the end of the Lord.' (Jas 5.11.) He means that Christians have seen the goal of utterly gracious love to which God's purposes are working. But there is an important sense in which the New Testament discloses the end of God in fulfilment only as it speaks of the 'death' of a God who could sustain any other confidence.

This was the point on which Dietrich Bonhoeffer insisted, and why he was able to see the squeezing out of the God of religion by the ineluctable advance of secularization not as the end of what Christianity means but in a real sense as its release. For the God Jesus reveals is the God who refuses to exist as the answer to men's unfulfilled needs or as the *deus ex machina* who can be relied on to be there when human powers fail. He declines such a role. He allows himself to be edged out of the world—on to the Cross.

The Cross was in the first place the death of God for Jesus himself : 'My God, my God, why has thou forsaken me?' (Mark 15.34). In so far as Jesus relied on God as a power to intervene, this was the end. For that God had failed even the one whom he had claimed as his 'Son.' But the Christian gospel affirms that God is to be found not in that projection of man's religious yearning—in 'the one above' who could have sent twelve legions of angels and didn't. He was on the Cross itself, 'reconciling the world to himself.' It was *here* that Love as the clue to everything was to be sought—not ' out there ' failing to prevent it, but in the midst of the evil triumphing over it. God, insists Bonhoeffer, is a God who dies on us—only to meet us on the Emmaus road if we are really prepared to abandon him as a long-stop and to find him, not at the boundaries of life where human powers fail, but at the centre, as 'the beyond in the midst.'

The end of God in fulfilment and hope has as its corollary for the New Testament a real end both to God and to hope. So, conversely, in our day, I believe, 'the death of God' as proclaimed (astonishingly) by Christians has as its complement—and corrective—a fresh awareness of his presence as the One who comes to us 'from the end,' that is, from ahead of us in history, beckoning us onward at the moving edges of growth and commitment. 'He is not here . . . he is going before you' (Mark 16.6-7): the angel's message at the empty tomb recurs as a refrain that runs through the pages of the Bible.

Such at any rate is a theme that seems to me worth exploring. Yes, God is dead, genuinely—if we expect him in the old habitations, mental or material. Yet he is not dead—if we are open to the signs of his appearing. And *an* area at least in which he is waiting and asking to be found is in a recovered sense of the future, or, rather, of the unrealized and unattainable in the present, representing the constantly open frontier where the spirit of man meets and is met by the Spirit of God.

But before proceeding to elaborate that, I would interject a word of balance and of warning. Eschatology is one direction from which the word and reality of God may perhaps come alive for men of our day. But, in the words which F. C. Happold quotes as the title to the Epilogue of his excellent Pelican book, *Religious Faith and Twentieth Century Man* : 'He who sees not God everywhere, sees him truly nowhere.' And I myself have argued strongly in *Exploration into God* for a 'panentheistic' position, in which God is in everything and everything is in God (as opposed to pantheism, which holds that God *is* everything and everything *is* God). Certainly one must not isolate eschatology or get it out of proportion (that way, indeed, lies the road to all the crankiness and sectarianism with which this particular field has ben littered). Yet it is not irrelevant that the most explicit Biblical text for the truth of panentheism, that God is 'all in all' (1 Cor. 15.28), occurs in a strongly eschatological context. For the Bible this is a truth about the End: it is expressed in the future tense. But, as we shall see, this does not mean, for the New Testament, that it is true only *after* everything else. It means that the truth about *everything* in Christ has an eschatological colouring.

It is all seen through 'the end of God.' That is why this particular aspect of Christian doctrine is not just one department, an appendix (as it has tended to become), but is decisive for a recovered awareness of the whole. With this in mind, therefore, I should like to urge the relevance of eschatology for understanding, and passing beyond, the death of God in our time.

I said earlier that the cry has gone up that 'God is dead' because either the word or the reality has died for many of our generation. In each case I believe that what has gone dead may yet live again for modern secular man if it can come to him across the unforeclosed frontier of the future.

First, I would cite two witnesses who were both profound believers in God but acutely aware of the difficulty of speaking of him within the context of our contemporary culture, which each entered into with such empathy.

The first is Paul Tillich, and the words of his I have in mind are ones that I quoted in a rather different connection in *Honest to God*:

> The name of this infinite and inexhaustible ground of history is *God*. That is what the word means, and it is that to which the words 'Kingdom of God' and 'Divine Providence' point. And if these words do not have much meaning for you, translate them, and speak of the depth of history, of the ground and aim of our social life, and of what you take seriously without reservation in your moral and political activities. Perhaps you should call this depth 'hope,' simply hope. For if you find hope in the ground of history, you are united with the great prophets who were able to look into the depth of their times, who tried to escape it, because they could not stand the horror of their visions, and who yet had the strength to look to an even deeper level and there to discover hope.[6]

---

[6] *The Shaking of the Foundations*, p. 59 (Pelican edition, p. 65f).

Hope is so near to the heart of the meaning of God that, like love, it can stand for it. At least it is a way in for those for whom the word 'God' does not have much meaning any longer. And as often as not it carries the overtones of the Biblical word 'endurance.' It is that which refuses to allow us to give up or sell out, which makes us go on believing or caring when despair or compromise would seem the only thing left. Such hope against hope may not require the word 'God.' But it may nevertheless be his 'word,' or the word for him—the indication that his reality is involved. The Bible is full of such 'signs' or acted parables of God's presence. There is a notable one in Jer. 32.6-44, where in an apparently hopeless situation, with the country irretrievably lost to the Babylonians and its leaders deported, the Prophet witnesses to the 'beyond' of faith by an act of political courage and economic madness in solemnly purchasing a plot of land from his cousin, with the full paraphernalia of witnesses and deeds. 'I knew,' he says, 'that this was the word of the Lord. . . . For thus says the Lord of hosts, the God of Israel : Houses and fields and vineyards shall again be bought in this land.'

The second passage I would quote is quite a different one from a great Christian humanist of the same generation, Nikos Kazantzakis, the author of *Zorba the Greek*. It comes from his autobiography, *Report to Greco*,[7] and starts not from history but from nature. Or rather, it speaks of that same on-going process of evolution which, when it becomes conscious of itself in man and begins to take a hand in its own destiny, we start to call history.

Blowing through heaven and earth, and in our hearts and the heart of every living thing, is a gigantic breath —a great Cry—which we call God. Plant life wished to continue its motionless sleep next to stagnant waters, but the Cry leaped up within it and violently shook its roots: 'Away, let go of the earth, walk!' Had the tree been able to think and judge, it would have cried,

[7] Pp. 291-2; quoted also in *Exploration into God*, pp. 101-2.

'I don't want to. What are you urging me to do!
You are demanding the impossible!' But the Cry, without
pity, kept shaking its roots and shouting, 'Away, let
go of the earth, walk!'

It shouted in this way for thousands of eons; and
lo! as a result of desire and struggle, life escaped the
motionless tree and was liberated.

Animals appeared—worms—making themselves at home
in water and mud. 'We're just fine,' they said. 'We
have peace and security; we're not budging!'

But the terrible Cry hammered itself pitilessly into their
loins. 'Leave the mud, stand up, give birth to your
betters!'

'We don't want to! We can't!'

'You can't, but I can. Stand up!'

And lo! after thousands of eons, man emerged, trembling
on his still unsolid legs.

The human being is a centaur; his equine hoofs are
planted in the ground, but his body from breast to head
is worked on and tormented by the merciless Cry. He
has been fighting, again for thousands of eons, to draw
himself, like a sword, out of his animalistic scabbard.
He is also fighting—this is his new struggle—to draw
himself out of his human scabbard. Man calls in despair.
'Where can I go? I have reached the pinnacle, beyond
is the abyss.' And the Cry answers, 'I am beyond. Stand
up!' All things are centaurs. If this were not the case,
the world would rot into inertness and sterility.

The Cry—it links with what the Bible speaks of as
'the call' of God, that evocative, purposive love, which

not only summons men to leave the securities and satisfactions of life about them, but ' calls the generations from the beginning ' (Is. 41.4) and indeed ' calls for the corn and increases it ' (Ezek. 36.29). But it links also with the cry of creation itself, the yearning sigh of all being for its goal, of which St. Paul speaks in Rom. 8.14-28. The cry is of God's Spirit within us—and indeed within all nature —calling us constantly out of ourselves and beyond ourselves in order to be ourselves. This is one of the great classical passages of Christian eschatology. It merits quoting in full from the New English Bible, because I believe that at several points[8] this version has allowed its true meaning to stand forth for the first time.

For all who are moved by the Spirit of God are sons of God.

The Spirit you have received is not a spirit of slavery leading you back into a life of fear, but a Spirit that makes us sons, enabling us to cry ' Abba! Father!' In that cry the Spirit of God joins with our spirit in testifying that we are God's children; and if children then heirs. We are God's heirs and Christ's fellow-heirs, if we share his sufferings now in order to share his splendour hereafter. For I reckon that the sufferings we now endure bear no comparison with the splendour, as yet unrevealed, which is in store for us. For the created universe waits with eager expectation for God's sons to be revealed. It was made the victim of frustration, not by its own choice, but because of him who made it so; yet always there was hope, because the universe itself is to be freed from the shackles of mortality and enter upon the liberty and splendour of the children of God. Up to

[8] Notably in making ' the Spirit ' the subject of the closing verse (v. 28)—instead of ' all things ' (K.J.V.) or ' God ' (R.S.V.). The Spirit is here, as indeed in everything, on both sides of the relationship, taking up *our* inarticulate groans (cf. earlier vv. 22-3) and translating them into prayer.

the present, we know, the whole created universe groans in all its parts as if in the pangs of childbirth. Not only so, but even we, to whom the Spirit is given as firstfruits of the harvest to come, are groaning inwardly while we wait for God to make us his sons and set our whole body free.

For we have been saved, though only in hope. Now to see is no longer to hope: why should a man endure and wait for what he already sees? But if we hope for something we do not yet see, then, in waiting for it, we show our endurance.

In the same way the Spirit comes to the aid of our weakness. We do not even know how we ought to pray, but through our inarticulate groans the Spirit himself is pleading for us, and God who searches our inmost being knows what the Spirit means, because he pleads for God's own people in God's own way; and in every-thing, as we know, he co-operates for good with those who love God and are called according to his purpose.

This Cry, this inexpungeable hope, corresponds to the reality of the transcendent that men point to when they speak of God. A previous age would instinctively have located it in another order above or beyond this. But ours is a generation which no longer starts its thinking, even about transcendence, from above[9]—from the meta-physical realities of a supernatural order. It works from the bottom upwards, rather than from the top downwards. It must take off and reach out from where it is. Its appre-hension of God comes, if it comes at all, in terms of an openness of this world, rather than in terms of a being who exists in some other world. The latter God is indeed dead

[9] See the excellent discussion on 'thinking from below' in contrast to 'thinking from above' and on 'transcendence' in Colin Williams, *op. cit.*, pp. 39-42, 75-88.

or dying: he belongs to an area of experience in which men no longer live, except peripherally.[10]

But can men to-day discern even that openness? Or is secular*ism* the only world-view possible—the world-view that takes the truth of secularization and makes it into a closed philosophy of life, as 'scient*ism*' does with the truth of science? I believe passionately that it is not the only possible option. I believe in God, in the transcendent, the unconditional, as a living, wide-open reality. He forms the living frontier, inside and out, of every aspect of man's being, of every particle in the universe. But I am also acutely aware of the task of *translating* transcendence for modern secular man. The traditional projections do so in terms of a mental picture of the universe he no longer shares and effectively make remote what is meant to be most real. My concern is therefore to start from some point or points of openness within experience that at least are real. I believe there are such places even for modern man. I would point to the unconditional in personal relationships and social justice, to the claim of integrity and the judgment of the sacred, to the ecstatic in 'peak experiences,' to 'the point of intersection of the timeless with time '[11] attested by artists and poets, musicians and mystics. But here I want to follow up a hint thrown out by Harvey Cox,[12] that the most significant area in which empirical, technological man is open to transcendence is the future.

This is *not* because it is the one frontier which he cannot close by his knowledge or control. That would be

[10] I have elaborated this in Chapter I of *Exploration into God*.
[11] T. S. Eliot, 'The Dry Salvages', *Collected Poems 1909-62*.
[12] In *The Secular City* (especially Chapter V and VI); *The Secular City Debate*, pp. 197-203; and 'The Death of God and the Future of Theology' in *The New Christianity* (ed. W. R. Miller), pp. 379-89. See also for further exploration in this direction: L. Dewart, *The Future of Belief*; R. Garaudy, *From Anathema to Dialogue*; J. Moltmann, *Theology of Hope*. These last three most significant books appeared too late for me to be able to take account of them in the text.

to locate God once again in the gaps, at the point of man's weakness and ignorance. It would be a case of God yesterday (now dead), God to-morrow, but never God to-day. No, it is because paradoxically, this is the point of man's strength. Man 'come of age' is man who takes responsibility for his world—for whom the future, even of his own genes, is no longer simply 'in the lap of the gods.' Such a God is dead. And the Christian joins in the celebration of his demise, for this is liberation.

But it is at this very point of his freedom that man hears 'the Cry,' the summons to transcend himself, to reach out into other worlds, to turn the wilderness into a watered garden, and break through every barrier external and internal. There is a bursting awareness of the potential in nature, and still more in man himself, that has lain so long locked up and idle. And this has created a new consciousness in twentieth-century technological man. It was William Hamilton, one of the 'God is dead' theologians, who made the point vividly for me, as he spoke of looking up at the night stars with his young son. While he was pondering, like Pascal, on the impotence of man before the terrifying silence of the infinite spaces, his boy broke in: 'Say, Dad, which are the ones we put up?' There is a confidence (directed towards the future rather than towards the gods), of which Hamilton himself has written under the engaging title 'The New Optimism—from Prufrock to Ringo.'[18] And of this theme the best presentation I know is Kenneth Boulding's *The Meaning of the Twentieth Century: The Great Transition.*

Of course, this could be the beginning of a new Promethean titanism. The potential, indeed, for evil and for disaster is immeasurably extended. The Christian will witness to this with a realism that measures both 'the greatness and the wretchedness of man.' A *self*-confidence is still as deceiving and as dangerous as ever. To base one's hope, to ground one's eschatology, in man and his perfectibility is the great illusion that prophets and reformers have known it to be.

[18] Reprinted in *Radical Theology and the Death of God*, pp. 157-69.

It is always the end of God, rather than the ends of man, that provides the surety.

But this is no reason for depreciating the great secular hopes of twentieth-century humanity. Indeed, the Christian with his awareness of what real, eternal, life is meant to be, must say even to modern man : 'Your hope is too small.' And that may be the most effective way of saying : 'Your God is too small.' To have articulated this for our generation is surely the great contribution of Teilhard de Chardin.[14] For at this point transcendence, the infinite horizon of life, encounters man in his strength and maturity and responsibility—in other words, in what the Bible speaks of as his call to 'sonship,' which is its figure not for childish dependence but for the freedom of adult manhood (see especially Gal. 4.1-7 and John 8.31-6).

Indeed, it is precisely here, if we have the eyes to see it, that the spirit of secular man and the Spirit of the God of the Bible touch most creatively. Harvey Cox makes the point that for the Biblical writers the characteristic 'place' of God, if we must localize him at all, is not 'out there' in space but 'ahead' of man in history.[15] He is the one who goes on before. His is the Spirit that from the beginning broods over the face of the waters, drawing all things out and up to light and life. He it is who calls the foundations of the earth and the heavens that they stand forth together; who summons Adam to response and responsibility; who challenges Abraham to go out, not knowing where he is going; who teaches his people to live as men that must be on their way in the morning; who precedes them in the cloud by day and the pillar of fire by night; who draws them on as pilgrims that have here no abiding city; who puts eternity into man's heart and teases him with a hope of a Messianic age.

[14] Particularly in *The Phenomenon of Man* and *The Future of Man*. See also the section of *pensées*, 'Humanity in Progress,' collected in his *Hymn of the Universe*.

[15] In this and the following paragraph I have adapted some material from *Exploration into God*.

And when the Messiah does come, he still calls men out to a Kingdom which within history is always 'at hand,' to a quality of life beyond their grasp. Constantly it is there before them,[16] just as he himself is on the road ahead (Mark 10.32) urging them to follow. And even at what appears to be the end, he again goes before them, first into Galilee, and then to the ends of the earth and the end of time. Once more the process starts afresh in the apostolic Church. Its whole life is directed towards the *parousia*, or presence, of Christ, viewed not as a static, appropriated reality but as a constant coming into the midst. And St. Paul's final testimony is typical of the craning hope on which the Bible closes: 'I do not consider that I have made it my own; but one thing I do, forgetting what lies behind and straining forward to what lies ahead, I press on towards the goal for the prize of the upward call of God in Christ Jesus' (Phil. 1.13-14). 'I am not yet perfect,' he says; yet the Christian's calling is to be *teleios* (Matt. 5.48), which means fundamentally not one who is morally perfect but one whose entire life is shaped by the *telos* or end of God in Christ.

Such is the Biblical perspective, in which the Church is called to be the avant-garde of the Kingdom, the eschatological community whose 'transcendent' life is to serve as the sign, within this age or *saeculum* (that is to say, in the midst of the secular), of the open future of man and of all creation's destiny. This is the process of 'hominization' and 'Christification' of which Teilhard de Chardin spoke, converging upon the 'Omega point' of that Love which all along has been drawing everything in freedom to itself.

And it is with a word of Teilhard's that I would end this chapter. 'The expectation of heaven,' he says, 'cannot remain alive'—or, in other words, God will stay dead, the transcendent cannot have reality—'unless it is incarnate. What body shall we give to ours to-day? That of a huge and *totally human* hope.'[17] By 'totally human hope' he

---

[16] The force of the verb in Matt. 12.28=Luke 11.20.
[17] *Le Milieu Divin*, p. 150. Italics his.

clearly does not mean one that is purely and simply human. He means one that sees nothing as lying outside the scope of an all-embracing divine humanism. And this introduces the other new context in which I would now wish to set what I first wrote nearly twenty years ago.

CHAPTER II

An Open Humanism

A few years ago the American religious magazine *The Christian Century* ran a series in which prominent churchmen and theologians were invited to say ' How my mind has changed.' This chapter might be given a similar heading.

As I indicated earlier, in *substance* I found that I wanted to alter remarkably little. Naturally I wanted to make—and have made—a number of corrections, omissions, and additions. Indeed, I could add much—if only because this theme of eschatology, of the Christian hope, has occupied a good proportion of my subsequent writing and research.[1] But to-day I should have to write it quite differently. For in manner of expression, as opposed to content, I could not say the same thing. And this is typical of how my mind has changed.

I find there are those who suppose that *Honest to God* changed everything : before that I was reasonably orthodox and conservative; since then I have believed less and less! But this, needless to say, is a complete over-simplification. As I dig up old sermons and articles I constantly surprise myself by coming across the essential ideas in *Honest to God* ten or more years earlier. In fact, I made it clear at the time that the book represented thoughts that had been collecting under the surface for a considerable period. Equally, I find I want to continue to say most of the things I said before—and I hope that the re-publication of this book will serve as further evidence of this. I have never thought of myself as standing anywhere but in the

[1] See ' The Christian Hope ' in *Christian Faith and Communist Faith* (ed. D. M. Mackinnon); *Jesus and His Coming*; *On Being the Church in the World* (Chapters I, XI, XII, and XIII); *Christ Comes in*; ' Resurrection in the N.T.' in *The Interpreter's Dictionary of the Bible* (Vol. 4.).

main stream of Christian orthodoxy, though usually on its radical edge. But to be a radical one must have roots, and deep roots. To cut oneself off from tradition is to wither and die.

What has changed—and *Honest to God*, or rather the tide on which it was borne along, has made the movement irreversible—is the way in which we can speak. We cannot go on saying the same things in the same way—or they will not be the same things. Equally, of course, they will not be precisely the same things when said in a new way. Christianity as formulated in Judaea of the first century or Alexandria of the third, by the Schoolmen of the thirteenth century or the Reformers of the sixteenth, in the age of the Enlightenment or the age of Automation, is not the same. The Christ who is the same yesterday, to-day, and for ever can only be so by becoming the contemporary of each generation—so that Bonhoeffer's question 'Who is Christ for us to-day?'[2] has to be answered afresh in every age.

To be more specific about the change that has occurred, it is partly a question of the cash-value, the meaning in empirical terms, of most of the words that have served as the counters of traditional theological exchange. Of these, the first and most fundamental is that of 'God' itself. We shall no doubt have to go on using the word, but it is increasingly necessary to clarify the reality to which we suppose it refers and to say how it functions. Doubt about the possibility of theological statements is a good deal more constricting than when I first wrote what is now the fourth chapter of this book.

Certainly there is a sense in which I can say that I believe less and less. So many of the theological propositions to which one is asked if one assents seem, increasingly, incapable of empirical verification one way or the other, and therefore devoid of much meaning. If I am asked, in the sense in which the questioner usually means it, 'Do you believe in life after death?' or 'Do you believe in the Second Coming?'—that is, 'What do you think is the state

[2] *Op. cit.*, p. 152.

of the individual five minutes, or five years, after death?'
'Do you think Christ will in any literal sense come back?'
—my only honest answer is, 'I do not and I cannot know.'
On many things I am a Christian agnostic. But that means 'a
Christian who does not know.' On the fundamental trust
of which these 'beliefs' are the projections I am unshaken.
It is simply that I do not see that we can have the evidence
for making many of the affirmations—or negations—in which
our forefathers so freely indulged, and nowhere more than
in the field of eschatology. (One has only to think of
purgatory, limbo, double predestination, reincarnation, mil-
lenarianism, the second death, to extend the list indefinitely.)
I understand the realities to which these ideas are, often
confusedly, trying to point, and I want to bring them all
to the judgment of the truth as I know it in Jesus. I would
continue to testify to the centrality and veracity for me of the
fundamental Biblical convictions and would wish to see
them interpreted still further in the direction which I began
to indicate in this book. That is why I am happy to give
it a new lease of life. At the same time I realize now how
easily I used the conventional language and the thought-
frame of traditional theism.

But the change is not simply one of expression—however
far reaching—but of perspective. I wrote *In the End, God*
. . . at a time when I was at my most right-wing in theology.
I never indeed went to any extreme in that direction. I was
not at any time a Barthian, however much all those of us
who grew up in the inter-war years are indebted indirectly
to the massive witness and theological integrity of Karl
Barth. The end of the Second World War saw us still in the
post-liberal reaction, in theology as in politics. It was an
age in which 'neo-orthodox' theology was in the ascendant,
and in my own thinking I owed most to Emil Brunner and
Reinhold Niebuhr (if one does not include the dominating
influence of a very different man, Martin Buber, on whose *I
and Thou* I did my Ph.D. thesis)[3]—though this book shows

[3] See further the Prologue to *Exploration into God*.

me disagreeing with Brunner on a most fundamental point.[4] We had also scarcely emerged from the period of the Resistance and the Confessing Church. It was an age in which thinking was conditioned by reaction to totalitarianism, whether of the Hitlerite or Stalinist variety. This had the effect of sharpening the edge of the Church over against the world and of stressing the hard core of the Gospel in its difference from the other religions and ideologies of the day. The fear was of erosion, appeasement, or what Roman Catholics would call indifferentism. James Moffatt wrote a book about that time called *The Thrill of Tradition*, and its title reflected a widely shared concern to let the pure gold of the deposit of Faith shine out from all that had overlaid it. If only one could allow the original Apostolic preaching, or the four-fold action-pattern of the Liturgy, or the essential ministry of the Church, or whatever, to stand forth in all its pristine power, it would be self-authenticating, at least to judge if not to convert.

One of the motives that prompted *In the End, God . . .* was the recognition that in the area of the Last Things the tradition was singularly failing to attract or engage. It was overlaid with so much that appeared to twentieth-century man a fantastic collection of lumber. My concern was to revitalize the dead myths and to show that they could speak with relevance and urgency to an age which under tribulation and persecution and the first impact of atomic destruction had had its hope shaken to the foundations. It was a concern which subsequently provided the focus of the second Assembly of the World Council of Churches at Evanston in 1954, preparation for which itself evoked some valuable clarifications of the Christian hope.[5]

All this tended to concentrate attention on isolating the distinctively Christian message. It was a fallow time

[4] See pp. 113-16 below.
[5] Notably E. Brunner, *Eternal Hope*; J. E. Fison, *The Christian Hope*; P. S. Minear, *Christian Hope and the Second Coming*; C. F. D. Moule, *The Meaning of Hope*.

for comparative religion, which belonged to what the Germans called *Religionsgeschichte* (the history of religions), whereas the Gospel was concerned with *Heilsgeschichte* (the history of salvation). It was a time when I personally was most influenced (though never without substantial reservations) by Oscar Cullmann, whose epoch-making *Christ and Time* had just appeared in the original. It reflected a break with the kind of thinking represented by half a century of Gifford Lectures on philosophical theology, many of which could have borne the title *God and Time*. This was a Christocentric, Biblicist view of the universe, deeply suspicious of philosophy and natural theology.

Above all it was profoundly suspicious of humanism— whether the old liberal humanism of the John Dewey tradition (where education was the handmaid of salvation) or the newer scientific humanism of which C. H. Waddington was the current English proponent (in which science and evolution were capable of supplying our ethics and seeing us through). Indeed, I am still not altogether happy with the word ' human*ism*.' In its current sense it is of surprisingly recent origin—dating back less than a hundred years. The term ' human*ist*' indeed has a long and honourable tradition, originating in the sixteenth century; and the first men to call themselves such were, of course, avowedly Christian. And in this distinction there lies, I sense, a difference of some importance. Humanism is an ' ism,' a system purporting to account for the whole in terms of a part. It is a self-contained interpretation of phenomena to the exclusion of other competing interpretations. And I am critical of all ' isms '—whether scientism, secularism, positivism, or even within my own ecclesiastical tradition, Anglicanism.[6]

But, in contrast with twenty years ago, I would now gladly accept the label (if label one must have) of Christian humanist. Indeed, Jacques Maritain was speaking long before *True Humanism* in his *humanisme intégral,* of which

[6] Also a term of nineteenth-century origin. The shapers of the Anglican tradition never thought of themselves as constructing any such system or ' ism.'

Christianity represents—not the closed humanism of man shut up to his own resources and values, but the humanism of man open to God and the Spirit, of humanity finding its norm and fulfilment in Christ.

Indeed, I would now judge it to be of vital importance, without blurring the edge of the distinctively Christian affirmation, to emphasize the solidarity of all those concerned for the humanity of man, whether or not they would base it on religious convictions. I should be far more open than I was to the positive contribution of non-Christian faiths and to the mystical tradition which flows across the boundaries of all religious organizations. Moreover, Bonhoeffer, with his talk of 'religionless' Christianity, has reminded us that there is likely to be as much affinity between the Christian estimate of man and secular humanisms of our day as between it and religious systems in which the sense of our co-humanity is weaker. Indeed, one finds in practice more ground for co-operation in the causes of social justice with secular humanists having a strong sense of responsibility for this age or *saeculum* than with other-worldly, individualistic, or non-politically minded Christians.

But in all this I would plead as strongly for an 'open' humanism as Michael Novak has pleaded, from within the well-protected citadel of Roman Catholicism, for an 'open' Church. A naturalistic humanism, in which man seeks to construct sand-castles of civilization within the order of an alien, impersonal nature that must eventually sweep them all away, seems to me as uninviting as ever. Unless the human individual and human society are grounded in a reality that transcends this material life, then all our efforts are simply whistling to keep up our courage before the dark driftings of the cosmic weather engulf us once more. For, if man is on his own in the universe, then beyond a brief span of years for the individual, or of millenia for the race, the future is irretrievably bleak. And it is not relieved for more than a short stay by the promise either of psychic survival or of terrestrial evolution. Unless human life is essentially response to a reality beyond itself from which

not even death can separate, then I see no hope for humanism
or for anything else. It is the achievement of Teilhard de
Chardin to have formulated this open humanism for our
generation in terms which make it accessible to those most
predisposed by their studies to interpret everything within
the processes of change and decay.

What is new and creative is the recognition that there
are indeed different 'perspectives' in humanism. There must
be dialogue here, and I believe that the Christian has a perspective which it is important that others should be able to
see and to share. This book then is re-offered as a contribution
precisely at a point where orthodox Christians seem so often
to have least to say to other humanists. I think back to a
couple of B.B.C. television programmes in 1964 on 'Heaven'
and 'Hell,' brilliantly presenting as the Christian tradition
almost everything that I should wish my humanist friends *not*
to believe of us. I could only recognize it with the very
heaviest discount as anything that I myself believe. Yet
it reflected only too accurately the eschatological scheme of
medieval Catholicism of which we are all the heirs. The
need to see the wood from the trees—and above all to cut
out the dead wood—is still as pressing as ever it was.

Finally, I would round off this section of new material
by saying two things about the perspective of this book—or
rather of the Christian hope as this book seeks to present it.

It is one of the book's central themes that all statements
about the End (whether of the individual or of history)
are fundamentally affirmations about God, and *vice versa*.
Everything that has happened since first I wrote it would
lead me to emphasize and deepen this interrelatedness. For
God is the End, as he is the Beginning, because he is the
eternal ground and power of all being, of whom and through
whom and to whom are all things. I should be less ready
now to speak of him as *a* Being existing in himself, out of
relation to what we can know of him. Not that I am suggesting
in the least that he is simply a function, a determinate, of
our petty existence. It is we who derive our beings and
our freedom unconditionally from his ultimate reality. Yet

what we can say of him (in such a way that anything could count for or against our statements) must be of what *we* experience of him as the depth of *our* existence, and not of him as he is outside or apart from this relationship.

But however much I might now wish to speak less of God, as it were, from his end of the relationship rather than ours, it is still in this relationship, utterly personal in its grace and claim, and in this relationship alone, that I would see the Christian's distinctive affirmation about the hope and meaning of life. 'This is eternal life,' says St. John in Jesus' prayer to the Father, 'that they may know thee the only true God and Jesus Christ, whom thou hast sent' (John 17.3). True life, life at its ultimate depth, consists in relatedness to this reality of love. And it is in this love, stronger than death, and not in anything in ourselves, that our trust resides. It is a love defined and vindicated for the Christian historically in the life, death, and resurrection of Jesus Christ, in whom he sees all the fullness of God dwelling bodily. But it is out of his *present* experience of this searching, fascinating, all-demanding while all-giving, reality, which will not let him go, that the Christian 'believes and trusts in the communion of saints, the forgiveness of sins, and resurrection to life everlasting.' It is a reality that comes to him with an unconditionality which 'nothing in death or life . . . in the world as it is or the world as it shall be' (Rom. 8.38, N.E.B.) can touch or terminate. If I really believed that it could be finished by a bus on the way home, then it would not have the unconditional character which I know it to have.

For the rest, I am prepared, like St. Paul, 'not to know anything' except 'Jesus Christ and him crucified' (1 Cor. 2.2), that is, once again, to be a *Christian* agnostic.[7] What happens to me after death I do not know. And precisely

[7] This text is usually quoted in support of a fundamentalist gospel suspicious of all 'free thinking.' It seems to me Paul's way of saying, with Professor Herbert Butterfield: 'Hold to Christ, and for the rest be totally uncommitted' (*Christianity and History*, p. 146; Fontana ed. p. 189).

what happened to Christ's body after his death I am also
prepared to leave open, without my conviction of his living
presence being affected. All I know is that nothing *depends*
on anything within the realm of flesh and blood (which for
the New Testament includes also 'the soul'). My hope
rests in nothing 'going on' or surviving dissolution, nor
in any speculation about the future or messages from beyond
the grave, but in the present reality of life in God. This is
not in the least to depreciate the value of serious psychical
research (as opposed to spiritua*lism*). Indeed, extra-sensory
perception is one of the open frontiers of our day, whose
exploration may perhaps tell us more of the unexplained
mysteries of human life and communication than any other.
But nothing for me hangs theologically on the results of
this or any of the other sciences—though these can constantly
serve to remind us that our God is too small.

This emphasis on the *present* ground of all eschatological
statements is the other main theme which shapes the perspective
of this book. It also marks a characteristically Biblical perspective in humanism.

One of the most commonly observed features of our age
is the apparent decline of interest in the so-called 'after
life.' Even preachers only refer to it peripherally, except
in Advent courses. In the younger generation I detect a
widespread scepticism and lack of conviction that it matters.
Young Christians too seem content to suspend judgment.
This is viewed with alarm and astonishment by many of
their elders, for whom everything would appear to turn
on what happens hereafter. An evangelical undergraduate
of an earlier generation confessed that if he did not believe
in a future life he would rape, steal, murder, and be a
drunkard. This strikes the contemporary humanist, whether
Christian or not, as not only incredible but immoral.[8] If
this is all that keeps a man responsible, then he is less than

[8] Cf. the passionate protest of Thomas Huxley in a letter to
Charles Kingsley (quoted by Leslie Weatherhead in *The Christian
Agnostic*, p. 32): 'As I stood behind the coffin of my little son

responsible. Morality must be self-authenticating or nothing; it must validate itself because it is true, whatever the consequences for the individual. And this holds whether or not it is conceived as grounded in anything transcendent. One of the remarkable features of the Old Testament is the unswerving faithfulness of patriarch, prophet, and psalmist to the will of Yahveh even when they saw no prospect before them but the pit. Similarly, the contemporary humanist recognizes an uncompromising wrongness, say, in the colour bar, even if it involves this day being his last. I believe this is a healthy perspective, and that in this matter we are truer to the Biblical outlook than many of our forefathers.

What the New Testament does is not to change this perspective, so that the focus of response and hope is transferred beyond the grave. But it proclaims as vindicated in Jesus what later Judaism had already sensed, namely, that if God is what he is then death *cannot* have the last word. His love continues to claim man unconditionally, whatever the outcome. But precisely because it is unconditional, it cannot be conditioned by anything; nothing in all creation can separate from it. And so, says St. Paul, 'if it is for this life only that Christ has given us hope, we of all men are most to be pitied' (1 Cor. 15.19; N.E.B.). The Gospel does not shift the centre of faith and obedience

---

the other day, with my mind bent on anything but disputation, the officiating minister read, as a part of his duty, the words, "If the dead rise not again, let us eat and drink, for tomorrow we die." I cannot tell you how inexpressibly they shocked me. Paul must have known that his alternative involved a blasphemy against all that was best and noblest in human nature. I could have laughed with scorn. What! Because I am face to face with irreparable loss, because I have given back to the source from whence it came the cause of a great happiness, still retaining through all my life the blessings which have sprung and will spring from that cause, am I to renounce my manhood, and, howling, grovel in bestiality? Why, the very apes know better, and, if you shoot their young, the poor brutes grieve their grief out and do not immediately seek distraction in a gorge.'

to some other world, but it declares it inconceivable that life should be limited by the death either of the individual or of the race. In such a perspective death simply ceases to occupy a decisive position. Nothing any longer turns on it. 'O Death, where is your victory? O Death, where is your sting?' (1 Cor. 15.55).

CHAPTER III

The Modern Mind

Nowhere, over the field of Christian doctrine, is the gulf between the Biblical viewpoint and the outlook of modern secularism so yawning as in the matter of eschatology. The whole New Testament prospect of a return of Christ, accompanied by the transformation of this world-order, a general resurrection, a final judgment, and the vindication of the sovereignty of God over heaven and earth, is regarded by the scientific humanist of the twentieth century as frankly fantastic. The Biblical narratives of the Last Things seem to him as incredible as the Biblical narratives of the First Things appeared to his grandfather a century ago. Or, rather, they are more incredible. For, whereas the Genesis stories, reinterpreted, could, it was found, be harmonized with the evolutionary picture, the Second Advent and its accompaniments appear to the modern a simple contradiction of all his presumptions about the future of the world, immediate or remote. And yet, despite its incompatibility with the modern outlook, the Biblical view of the Last Things, unlike that of the First, has hardly stirred a ripple of controversy. The entire Christian eschatological scheme has simply been silently dismissed without so much as a serious protest from within the ecclesiastical camp.

This could only have happened if the Church's doctrine at this point had become not merely incredible, but irrelevant. 'The storm in a Victorian tea-cup,' as Professor C. E. Raven called the previous controversy, at least proved that an intensely live issue was at stake. But for contemporary thought to-day the Christian doctrine of the Last Things is dead, and no one has even bothered to bury it. To appreciate why this is so, it is necessary to take account of two changes in the secular outlook which distinguish the mind of the twentieth century from that of the nineteenth.

The first change would appear perhaps to make the Christian teaching seem more rather than less relevant. It is the fact that it is very much easier to-day than it was for our grandfathers to reckon seriously upon the end of the world. The nineteenth-century scientists may have known well enough the chilling prospects for the future of this earth under the second law of thermo dynamics. But it was not a knowledge that modified in any serious way the general optimism of the Victorian outlook. The end of the world was far away, and human society had ample time to reach the goal of its progress before that need be reckoned with. Moreover, it was only a limited number of people who really believed that, in the most significant sense, this was the end. The majority retained enough of the Christian heritage to doubt, even if things should prove to go out ' not with a bang but a whimper,' whether it seriously mattered. But to a generation brought up, not merely to the conclusions of the laboratory, but, more importantly, to its perspectives and horizons, the picture of the last state of our planet colours, or pales, much of its more sober thinking.

But to-day, of course, it is nothing so gradual or remote as the cold processes of entropy (or the now-favoured probability of a scorched earth, as the sun converts more and more of its hydrogen into helium) that has forced men to reckon again with the end of the world as a serious possibility. Scientists may deny the likelihood of the disintegration of this planet, or even of the total annihilation of human life, as the result of uncontrolled chain reaction from atomic fissure. The layman is left to place what confidence he can in such assurances and to derive from them what comfort he may. But whether the eclipse of human history be total or merely partial, the live possibility, not to say probability, of such an event in the foreseeable future, has brought back the issues of eschatology not simply to the laboratory but to the lobby.

All this might, as was said, seem to betoken a new relevance and promise a new hearing for the Christian message of the End. And there have not lacked those who in their preaching and evangelism have sought to turn the situation to account.[1] But this is to reckon without the second great change that has come over the nineteenth-century prospect.

Up to the end of the last century, and well into this, men were convinced that it was natural to seek the clue to the course of history in its final stage. That was an assumption which was foreign to the ancient world, except to the Jews and to such as had come under Zoroastrian influence. But with the spread of Christianity it became one of the accepted axioms of Western civilization. The modern belief in progress is, as has often been said, a Christian heresy, a secularized version of Hebraic eschatology. As long as this belief persisted, it was still to the end of things that men looked to find the meaning and justification of the whole. So much was this so, that, from the eighteenth century onwards, political theorists were happy to speak, as Christianity with its dimension of eternity had never done, as though every generation except the last could be regarded as a means to an end, provided that that last generation did obtain the promise. The logical conclusion of this assumption can be seen in Marxist thought, where the eschatological element is strong.[2] If every generation is a means to an end, then so is every individual in it—and so he can be treated. But, pursued ruthlessly to its secular conclusion or not, the assumption that it was legitimate to interpret history in terms of a goal was all but universally accepted.

To-day that presumption is disappearing. The final genera-

[1] 2 Pet. 3.10, for instance, provides an admirable 'atomic' text: 'The day of the Lord will come as a thief; in which the heavens shall pass away with a great noise, and the elements shall be dissolved with fervent heat, and the earth and the works that are therein shall be burned up.' To save a good deal of unprofitable labour I have kept the Biblical quotations in the older material in this book, where the sense is not affected, in the Revised Version (American Standard Version) in which I originally cited them. Writing today, I should naturally used the Revised Standard Version or the New English Bible.

[2] See my essay 'The Christian Hope' in *Christian Faith and Communist Faith* (ed. D. M. Mackinnon).

tion, far from being the favoured one, will simply be the unlucky one, either as it is called upon to endure natural conditions increasingly insupportable for human life, or as it has to witness the final agonies of racial suicide. Special value or significance attaches to the last term of a process only when the whole is thought to be purposive. Apart from a belief in teleology there can be no true *telos* or climax, but only a stopping, a cessation, a petering out. In this case, any term in the series becomes as important—or as meaningless—as any other. And in so far as men to-day have lost a conception of the end of history as more than cessation, whether lingering or catastrophic, they must fail to see any relevance whatever in a doctrine of last things. For the last things, on this reckoning, have no more significance for the understanding of the world than the penultimate, prepenultimate, or any other. It is for this reason that the gulf between the Church's teaching on eschatology and secular thought is wider to-day than ever before. Men now may have a more lively expectation of an end. But the decisive factor is whether they think of that end as purposive, not whether they believe it to be near. To the nineteenth century, the Christian scheme may have seemed incredible— an improbable answer to an intelligent question; to the twentieth it appears blankly irrelevant—the question itself has become meaningless. For, without some kind of belief in teleology, there can be no eschatology.

In an attempt at communication especially designed to speak to him modern man would frankly not expect to be presented with a book on the Last Things. For, however well-disposed he may be towards Christianity as a whole, he regards this particular department of it for the most part as dead wood. He might perhaps be prepared for a book on the future life, which is the only part of the traditional content of Christian eschatology in which the secular world retains a flicker of interest. And it does that, in so far as it does it, only because this doctrine has in modern teaching been lifted entirely out of its original framework of cosmic eschatology. How far in consequence this isolated fragment

has remained recognizably Christian is another matter, and
one that will require further discussion.

But even such interest as attaches to the question of
an after-life is notoriously weak in the modern world,
except when it is artificially stimulated in time of war. And
even here the second World War differed from the first
in revealing a much less active concern about the state of
the departed and a far more widespread spirit of fatalistic
indifference. About a question which touches every individual
so closely, and presses, one would think, yet the more urgently
in an age of destruction, the modern man is blandly un-
concerned. In his own jargon, he just couldn't care less.

What is the reason for all this? Ultimately, no doubt,
the fact that for the mass of his generation 'God is dead.'[8]
It is no accident that widespread atheism and a refusal to
believe in a life after death of any kind (both of them
phenomena unknown except in recent times) should have
made their appearance together. But, more immediately,
there is another cause.

Short of the ultimate issue of belief or disbelief in the
Christian God, the most fundamental fact which a writer
on Christian eschatology must face is that men to-day have
lost valid grounds for believing any statement about eschatology in any form. Deep down, contemporary scepticism may
doubtless be traced to irreligion; but to the sceptics themselves it is a question of *evidence*. The initial problem for
anyone approaching the subject is, therefore, epistemological.

What grounds are there for making any assertions about
eschatology which may reasonably claim to be true? Until
a hundred years ago or so such statements were thought to
rest securely, like other theological truth, on the twin foundations of revelation and reason. Time was when the future
prospects both of the individual and of the world could
be asserted with confidence on the authority of infallible
propositions of Holy Writ and the necessary postulates of
rational thinking. To-day that confidence has been almost

---

[8] It is interesting to me on reading it through to find that this
phrase occurred in the first edition of 1950.

entirely shattered. In matters eschatological, perhaps more than in any other department, the modern generation believes neither in the inerrancy of Scriptural statement nor in the validity of metaphysical thought. The whole edifice in which our forebears lived and hoped has collapsed with the crumbling of its epistemological foundations. The dark paths of the future have been abandoned to 'the astrologers, the star-gazers, the monthly prognosticators' (Is. 47.13), who, to-gether with the Theosophists, Spiritualists, Seventh Day Adventists, Jehovah's Witnesses, British Israelites, Christa-delphians, The Panacea Society, and the rest have stepped in to answer for the modern man Kant's third great question, 'What may I hope for?', to which Kant himself first caused men to doubt whether there might be a rational answer. And even those who do not go all the way to Endor have ceased to believe that assertions about the hereafter comprise more than a web of speculation, in which any statement is as likely, or as unlikely, to be true as any other. You may not pay your money, but you still take your choice. Christians themselves have lost confidence in their ability to give a bottom to their hopes which is more solid than sanctified wishful thinking. Even to the theologian the field of eschatology must appear the least amenable to those canons of induction and verification whereby his discipline, like any other science to-day, must substantiate its claim to give valid knowledge.

Before anything can be said, then, of the content of Christian eschatology, it is necessary to enquire afresh into its credentials. Ours is a day when the most significant Biblical theology is soaked through with eschatology. Its rediscovery has transformed and quickened our understanding of the gospel of Jesus and the apostolic church. If this new light is to break through into Christian doctrine and have any chance of touching secular thought, modern man has first to be convinced that the whole eschatological viewpoint, accepted without question by the New Testament writers, has any validity or relevance for the twentieth century. Unless this task of apologetic is successfully performed, we

shall be left, as Albert Schweitzer was, to make the best
of a situation where Biblical theology requires us to interpret
the Gospel in categories that are confessedly fantastic and
false for the modern world. And to rest there is either to
abandon the Gospel as dated and irrelevant, or to sever it
from all ties to its historical foundation. And the latter,
despite Schweitzer's heroic example, is equally to sound its
knell. For an unhistorical mysticism of ' the spirit of Jesus '
may be magnificent, but it is hardly catholic Christianity.

Moreover, whether men hear or whether they forbear,
the eschatology of the Christian gospel should be capable of
addressing this generation with a genuine relevance. Never
since the first century have men been so conscious of living
in the last times. ' "We live in an apocalyptic age "—
one hears from people who do not believe in any apocalypse
whatsoever.'[4] But in this century the Church has been
faced by people who *do* believe in apocalypses—the great
secular myths of Fascism, Nazism, and Communism, each
with its own eschatology of history. These myths have come
up like thunderstorms against the wind. In an intellectual
atmosphere slowly stifling all forms of teleology, these
vast, irrational cyclones have swept everything before them.

For men have found that they cannot live without an
eschatology. This recognition has come as the last stage
of a progressive disillusionment. The age which began at
the Renaissance confidently believed that it had overcome the
choice of having to decide between the Hebraic faith in a
God of history and the Classical acceptance of a God of
nature, between, that is to say, an ultimate interpretation of
the world in terms of *divine purpose* and an ultimate
interpretation of the world in terms of *natural process*. The
one gave goal and direction, but seemed indemonstrable;
the other looked scientific, but took the meaning out of
everything. With triumphant optimism, it put its trust in
the universe as itself a *purposive process*. An immanent
purposiveness could be relied on to see history through to

[4] Quoted from Berdyaev by E. Lampert, *The Apocalypse of History*,
p. 12.

an end which would not put human values to shame. This secular providence was understood in many forms : by some in terms of immanent spiritual forces, by others in the evolutionary categories of biology, by others again, including both the Manchester and the Marxist schools, in terms of economic law. But though the path of progress might run straight or dialectically, it was generally assumed that a pattern of advance was there to find, could men but detect and obey it. Freedom, as Marx insisted, lay in the recognition of necessity.

But the shattering of this confidence led to the rediscovery that history purely as nature, as process, could of itself guarantee no purpose. Spegler's *Decline of the West* (1918), with its return to a frankly naturalistic and cyclical interpretation of the birth and decay of civilizations, itself marked the end of a cycle. He spoke for a generation of men upon whom it seemed that history had defaulted, who had indeed seen the righteous forsaken and the poor man begging his bread. But men were soon to find they could not live in this waste land of resignation and despair, without a god or hope in the world. Spengler is himself symptomatic in that he was forced to go on to write another book, less well known, but whose title speaks for itself—*The Hour of Decision.* It was written to welcome the Nazi revolution of 1933.

For twentieth-century man has not been able to remain content with meaninglessness. If he cannot find meaning, he must create it. 'We have created our myth,' declared Mussolini at Naples in 1922. 'The myth is a faith, it is passion. It is not necessary that it shall be a reality. It *is* a reality by the fact that it is a goad, a hope, a faith, that it is courage. Our myth is the nation, our myth is the greatness of the nation.'[5]

Here is the man-made substitute for an end of history, which is no longer an attempt at a rational interpretation

[5] Quoted by Charles Smyth in 'Christianity and the Secular Myths,' *Theology*, October, 1949. I have paraphrased some sentences from this in the following paragraph.

of the direction of events, but a pattern to mould them. The point is not whether it is true, but whether it can be made to be true; it will be true if it can enlist the emotional and volitional drive necessary to turn it into a reality. An age which had given up believing that its hope would work because it was true (because, that is, it was written into the universe or grounded in God) succeeded in persuading itself that it must be true if it could be made to work, if a particular pattern—be it the New Roman Empire, the Reich that would last for a thousand years, the great Experiment of the U.S.S.R.—could be imposed upon events, and imposed by any methods.

The end of all this was a final disbelief in providence, either divine or secular; it was an attempt to *be* providence, to stamp one's own pattern and end on history. It was a last catastrophic effort to stave off return from the discredited Baalim of nature to the God of history. The hour was at hand when Christian eschatology would reassert itself with pressing relevance. Out of the darkened skies the strange, familiar words of the New Testament came again like thunder-claps to the Churches of the persecution. 'The end of all things is at hand' (1 Pet. 4.7); 'Little children, it is the last hour: and as ye heard that antichrist cometh, even now have there arisen many antichrists, whereby we know that it is the last hour' (2 John 1.18). Christians in cellars and concentration camps sensed again something of what it meant to live with the prayer, 'Amen: come, Lord Jesus.' There was a new expectancy and a new urgency abroad which might be felt wherever the Church was being the Church.

But if the Spirit is to be free to course men's minds, there is much mental lumber to be shifted and a deal of re-translation to be done.

CHAPTER IV

The Truth of the Ultimate

What are the grounds of eschatological statement, for saying anything valid about the possible end either of the individual or of the world? That is the basic question. But first it is necessary, in this generation, to go further back still. For the prevailing scepticism does not extend merely to the possibility of valid theological statement about the Last Things; it doubts whether any certain knowledge can be afforded by theology at all. Contemporary opinion supposes that the theologian occupies himself in argument and speculation about matters which lack any definite foundation of proof whatever. Precisely in the same way as the astrologer may spend a lifetime elaborating theories and predictions which to him are entirely convincing and self-consistent, and yet whose basic assumption (namely, that the course of the stars influences human destiny) is entirely unproven and improbable, so everything in the theologian's scheme is thought to rest upon an act of blind acceptance which disqualifies any of his conclusions from possessing the status of scientific knowledge.

In the days when all sciences were deductive, the theologian could perhaps be content with such a conception of his subject as underlies this criticism—namely, that it is a corpus of knowledge deduced from a number of revealed propositions which themselves are taken on faith as divine and therefore infallible. At least his initial presuppositions, attested, as he believed, by the witness of miracle and prophecy and confirmed independently by the natural reason, rested on grounds more convincing that those of the astrologers, alchemists, and other of his contemporaries.

But to-day this conception of theology as a deductive science of revelation must go. And that for two reasons. First, if persisted in, such a definition would preclude the claim of theology to any kind of knowledge that would be recognized as valid by the standards of modern critical science. To some this may not seem to matter. But theology has always made claim to be in some sense a science; and to abandon it completely at this hour is the mark either of a very bold or of a very foolish apologist. But there is a still more weighty reason. It is that over recent generations theologians themselves have come to see that such a definition is actually a false description of their own task and discipline.

One of the significant accomplishments in theology in the last generation has been Alan Richardson's achievement in giving definitive expression to this change.[1] It is a change so important, and so little understood outside the ranks of theology, that a repetition of his main points may be pardoned. He is concerned to vindicate theology as an empirical discipline which uses a method at all points comparable with that of the other inductive sciences. Its data, he insists, are as objective and indisputable as those of physics or biology—namely, the facts of 'Christian existence in history and to-day, . . . all that appertains to the believing and witnessing Christian community . . . both in the past and in the present . . . Like any other science, theology deals with the facts of human experience; it does not (as many apparently suppose) deal with hypothetical objects, or things about which there is a reasonable possibility of doubt.'[2]

The Christian theologian's material is historical fact—namely a persistent community of faith owing its existence to a series of events in history interpreted as acts of God. Faced with this fact, the theologian's first task, like that of any other scientist, is critical. He has to examine the history and documents on which this community and its faith rest, and to study the development of its life and belief. When he passes from the critical to the constructive part of his work (the department known as ' systematic theology '), his method is equally inductive. He does not start from

[1] See his *Christian Apologetics*, Preface and Chapter II.
[2] *Op. cit.*, p. 50.

certain texts or credal statements which must be accepted on
faith as indisputably true, and from them spin a system
of dogmatics. Rather, he begins with the Church's life and
proclamation as set out in its documents and living institu-
tions; he examines the understanding of revelation which
these presuppose; and he then seeks to formulate such general
statements about God and his relation to man as will account
for the facts under examination without explaining them away.
In doing this he is doing exactly the same as any other
scientist who formulates a hypothesis to co-ordinate and
explain the phenomena he is investigating. His hypotheses
must submit themselves to precisely the same test of verification in the light of the total evidence, and will possess the
same provisional authority. Within theology too there are
indeed certain formulations which may be said to possess
the status of scientific ' law,' being hypotheses which have
stood the test of generations. But ultimately every statement
of doctrine, like every ' law ' of nature, is open to revision
in the light of a fresh understanding of the evidence, past or
present. (Theories of the Atonement provide a good illustration in Christian theology of constant readjustment to meet
factors in experience to which less than justice has been done.)

The formulations of theology, therefore, about God, eschatology or anything else may thus be seen to be neither free
speculation, nor dogmas imposed by ecclesiastical authority,
but attempts to articulate and account for in the most scientific
manner possible the existence, life, and proclamation of the
Christian Church. And about this existence, life, and proclamation there can be no real doubt.

The conclusions of theology have, of course, a scientific and
not a metaphysical validity. It is not the task of theology to
say whether belief in God is ultimately true, any more than
it is within the scope of physics to pronounce the metaphysical
status of the phenomena it investigates. Science is not concerned with ultimate realities. What the scientist does is
to take the basic data of experience and try to analyse, co-
ordinate, and explain this in terms of proximate (rather than
ultimate) causation. His conclusions, in so far as his method

is genuinely scientific, are valid in providing 'knowledge about' the subject which is indispensable and reliable. But they do not give, nor can they ultimately prove or disprove, the direct 'knowledge of' given in immediate awareness.

Precisely the same limitations apply to theological as to every other type of scientific knowledge. If 'science' (i.e. the natural sciences) cannot disprove God, then neither can science (theology) prove him.[8] Each of the sciences in its investigation of the phenomenon of *belief* in God may adduce facts relating to the proximate causation of that belief (father-complexes, economic conditioning, historical events, etc.) which may result in deepening, modifying, or destroying that belief in different men or generations. But none of these facts can prove or disprove the ultimate reality of God.

Christian theology starts with a certain complex of beliefs and practices embodied in the historic community of the Christian Church. It cannot prove or disprove them. It cannot make metaphysical judgments about the ultimate truth of its doctrine. It cannot, for instance, on the subject of the Last Things, assert that such and such *will* be the ultimate issue of the universe. What it can and must do is to formulate what doctrines of the End are involved in the understanding of God and the world necessary to explain and account for the Christian phenomenon.

With this general introduction on the nature and status of theological truth, we must now go on to consider in more detail its particular application to statements about eschatology.

Deductive theology began by assembling the pronouncements of the Bible or ecclesiastical authority on the subject of the Last Things. These it accepted at their face value and proceeded to harmonize as best it might into a body of systematic doctrine. Such a procedure is to-day impossible. The datum from which a scientific theology begins is not a number of propositions which must be received uncritically as inerrant.

[8] The traditional 'proofs' of the existence of God are part of a whole understanding of theology as a deductive science (like mathematics) and assume that God can be demonstrated like a theorem of Euclid.

It is, as we have said, a community of faith grounded in a certain revelation of God. Now, if this revelation is analysed, it is found to be understood by the Bible (the accepted norm of the Church's belief) as imparted, not as proposition, but as presence. It is not the communication of oracles about things in heaven, on earth, and under the earth, past, present, and future; rather, it is encounter with the living God, who discloses himself for what he is in the act of answering man's need and demanding his obedience in the here and now of his personal and social existence. It speaks to him of a Presence and therefore of the present, of an insistent succour and demand confronting him for acceptance or rejection. All revelation is of a now and for a now. It is not in itself information about the past or the future.[4]

Such an understanding of revelation might appear effectively to preclude any significant theological statement about either the beginning or the end of the world. For revelation is seen as God speaking to particular men and generations through the events of their day of *present* mercy and *present* judgment. It is no longer the communication to Moses of information about the first day of history nor to Daniel of predictions about its last.

But the difficulty is only apparent, as Alan Richardson has pointed out with reference to the doctrine of creation.[5] The prophetic understanding of Yahweh as the Lord of history, given in the encounter of particular historical situations and for those situations, contained within it the knowledge of a God almighty over all situations, places, and times, the Lord and Creator of heaven and earth. Similarly, such an understanding carried with it a conviction of the ultimate sovereignty of God over the purpose and end of history. Statements of the First and Last Things are not independent ' revelations' given to satisfy human curiosity, nor are

[4] This doctrine of revelation, here summarily stated without argument, may well turn out to be one of the ' assured results' of modern scientific theology. It is that accepted, for instance, by such writers as William Temple, Emil Brunner, John Baillie, and Alan Richardson.

[5] *Op. cit.*, pp. 152f.

they free speculation. They are derived from the total appre-
hension of God given in *present* encounter with men of
succeeding generations. Consequently, the Bible's account
of Creation expresses itself as *part* of its primal awareness of
God: ' In the beginning, God . . ." In the same way, all its
eschatological assertions are likewise ultimate convictions
about *God*. This provides at once the ground and the criterion
for every Christian statement about the Last Things. Theological doctrine in this field is neither the co-ordination of
revealed propositions, nor the product of inspired or inspiring
speculation of which the only test is subjective. It is the
formulation of statements about the final sovereignty of
God as it must be understood if the data of Christian
existence are to be scientifically explained. It is the explication
of what must[6] be true of the end, both of history and of the
individual, if God is to be the God of the Biblical faith.
All eschatological statements can finally be reduced to, and
their validity tested by, sentences beginning: ' In the end,
God . . .'

An example of the fundamental nature of eschatological
statement as inference from present conviction of God is
provided by the only argument which Jesus is known to have
used to attest a future life. His assurance of it rested
completely on his present knowledge of the living God:
' He is not the God of the dead, but of the living' (Mark
12.27). In the same way, the Psalmist's hope, 'Thou shalt
not suffer thy beloved one to see corruption' (Ps. 16.10;
R.V. marg.), is founded on the known realities of the
nature of God and his relation to man—namely, that,
in the words of the hymn, ' He changeth not, and thou
art dear.' Indeed, every statement of Christian eschatology,
whether of the end of the individual or of the world,

[6] This ' must,' as was explained, is a scientific rather than a
metaphysical necessity. The formulations of theology, here as elsewhere, are hypothetical rather than final. But they are hypothetical,
not in the sense that they are speculative guesses, but in the
strictly scientific sense that they are hypotheses which require to be
verified, and can be verified, objectively, by reference to the data
to be explained.

is an inference from some basic truth in its doctrine of God, and must be judged and tested accordingly. False ideas of the Last Things are direct reflections of inadequate views of the nature of God.[7]

A clear illustration of this principle may be seen in the remarkable transformation that overtook Christian eschatology almost as soon as the ink of the New Testament was dry. And it affects the centre of interest or pivotal point of the entire subject.

The interest of the modern man in Christian eschatology, if he has any interest at all, centres in the fact and moment of death. He wants to know whether he will survive it and in what form; he wants to know what he is to expect on ' the other side,' what heaven will be like, whether there is such a place as hell, and so on. But it comes as a shock to realize how foreign is this perspective, which we take for granted, to the whole New Testament picture upon which Christianity is supposedly based.

For in the New Testament, the point around which hope and interest revolve is not the moment of death at all, but the day of the Parousia, or appearance of Christ in the glory of his Kingdom. Moreover, this is, first and foremost, a hope not for the dead, but for the living. The doctrine of the resurrection of the dead is formulated by St. Paul almost as an after-thought to meet the problem raised by that *minority* of Christians who had already died prior to the Parousia. Indeed, life after death is one of those subjects which gains even the limited space accorded it in the New Testament writings because it had *not* had a central place in the original Preaching and had since become

[7] Cf. H. R. Mackintosh, *Immortality and the Future*, p. 109: ' It is a just and illuminating thought that every system of theology should be read backwards at least once, commencing with the last things, since it is in the conclusion we find the truest index of the whole.' This test needs to be qualified by the recognition, which he himself quote (ibid, p. 111) from R. H. Charles, that ' eschatological beliefs are universally the last of all beliefs to be influenced by the loftier conceptions of God ' (*Immortality* (Drew Lecture), p. 9).

a matter of controversy. But even as, with the passage of time, the spiritual majority within the Church began to pass from the living to the dead, the centre of interest and expectation continued, right through the New Testament period, to be focused upon the day of the Son of man and the triumph of his Kingdom in a renovated earth. It was the reign of the Lord Jesus with all his saints that engaged the thoughts and prayers of Christians, not their own prospects beyond the grave. The hope was social and it was historical.

But as early as the second century A.D. there began a shift in the centre of gravity which was to lead by the Middle Ages to a very different doctrine. Whereas in primitive Christian thinking the moment of the individual's decease was entirely subordinated to the great day of the Lord and the final judgment, in later thought it is the hour of death which becomes decisive. It is *that* after which no repentance is possible, it is *that* which determines the destination of the soul, and it is *that* which supersedes the consummation of history as the main object of the believer's concern. The traditional ' four last things ' which stand at the end of the individual's life (death, judgment, heaven, and hell) take the place of the great Last Thing, or *Eschaton*, which closes everything.

If we ask what caused this astonishing transformation from a cosmic eschatology centring in the transformation of the universe at the last day, to an individualistic eschatology, centring in the fixing of personal destiny at the hour of death, the answer is to be found in a shift in the doctrine of God. The former eschatology derives from the Hebraic view of a God to whom time is important for the bringing to maturity of a purpose which includes and gives meaning to the whole process of history. Its climax, therefore, is the grand fulfilment of this cosmic design. The latter eschatology derives from the Hellenic view of a God to whom time is irrelevant except for bringing to perfection individual souls in and through the discipline of a material order that is itself doomed to destruction. The climax here is no longer cosmic. It comes separately for each individual at the

moment when he passes from this material order. For the state
in which he leaves it fixes his eternal destiny. Henceforward
he is capable only of purgation, not of change or decision.
For only matter and that which is in matter can change.[8]

Not only does this shift of emphasis represent a radical
change in doctrine of God in respect of his relation
to history, but it also reflects a hardening in the understanding of his essential character. The New Testament continually stresses the need for decision here and now and
without delay, but it does not give to the moment of death
the overriding significance which it later acquires. On
the one hand, it asserts that a man must make up his mind
'now,' 'while it is called "to-day"'. It does not say:
'any time before death.' The moment, the opportunity for
decision, may in fact be lost before death. And, on the
other hand, it never dogmatizes to the extent of saying
that after death there is no further chance. Indeed it
could not do so without limiting quite intolerably the inexhaustible love of God. No being who had an *infinite*
concern for the salvation of every soul could possibly be
conceived as saying in effect: 'Unless you turn to me by
the age of seventy, or seven, or seven weeks, I cannot give
you a further chance.' A God like that is either at the mercy
of death or he is not the God of the parable of the Prodigal
Son. To be content with the individual eschatology of later
Western Catholicism is to betray a sub-Christian view of the
fatherhood of God.

But while theological assertions about the beginning and
end of things are, in their essential content, derived from
present awareness of the living God, the *form* in which they
are expressed—that which makes them descriptions of the
past and future and not of the present—has yet to be
discussed. This form is *myth*. Again, it is important to
establish precisely what is mean by the term. For to the
contemporary mind it stands as the exact antithesis of
scientific fact—mere legend and fairy story. Consequently,

[8] Cf. O. C. Quick, *The Gospel of the New World*, pp. 70-3.

the eschatology of the Bible, inevitably involved as it is with myth, is dismissed by many as a kind of fantasia.

Myth of some kind is employed in many sciences when description is required where direct evidence is unobtainable. Physics, for instance, produces a myth or model to explain the basic constitution of matter, for the purposes of translating into some concrete imaginable picture what can accurately be stated only in formulae. The truth of the formulae does not depend on the later verification by sense-experience, if that were possible, of the myth or model. In the same way, modern psychology finds a vast amount of myth indispensable for describing the phenomena with which it is dealing. But it does not for one moment imagine that the truth of these phenomena depends on the actual reality of the Archetypes or the Censor, or the numerous figures, such as Eros and Thanatos, by which it seeks to explain the forces which battle for control of the psyche.

Theology too employs myth in the same way. It uses it for the purpose of translating its fundamental understanding of God, given and verified in present experience, into terms of the primal and ultimate, where it *must* apply and yet where direct evidence is, in the nature of the case, unobtainable. The truth of its myths, as of those of physics and psychology, depends entirely on that of the basic assertions which they embody—on whether, that is to say, the physical formula or the theological doctrine of God is one that is scientifically valid. Their truth does not depend on the mythical representations themselves being scientifically or historically accurate. Neither the myths of Genesis nor of Revelation set out to be *historical* reconstructions, i.e. literal accounts of what did, or what will, happen. As history they may be entirely imaginary, and yet remain theologically true. The only test of a myth is whether it adequately represents the data to be explained. It can never be proved false by showing, for example, that Eros and Thanatos, Adam and Eve, Gog and Magog, are not historical personages : there is nothing that requires that they should be. There may be instances where a particular myth gives a misleading picture of reality and has therefore to be modified or discarded. (Physics, for instance, has abandoned the myth of the Ether for this reason.) And certainly there are cases, particularly in theology, when a literalistic understanding of the myth has been allowed to distort the real truth for which it stands.

All this will recur for consideration later. Here we are simply concerned with myth as a form of scientific expression and more directly with its relation to eschatological truth. For it is not always sufficiently recognized that the eschatological statements of the Bible are of this nature, in precisely the same way as its narratives of the Creation and Fall. They are neither inerrant prophecies of the future nor pious guess-work. They are necessary transpositions into the key of the hereafter of knowledge of God and his relation to men given in the revelatory encounter of present historical event. The particular character of a myth (e.g., its presupposition of a 'three-decker' universe) is governed by the current assumptions of a particular age and place, and is not merely speculative; it is scientific in the sense already described.

CHAPTER V

The Ultimacy of Truth

Every truth about eschatology is *ipso facto* a truth about God. That is valid for all religions. But for the Judaeo-Christian religion the converse is also true; namely, that every statement about God is *ipso facto* an assertion about the end, a truth about eschatology.

This follows directly from the basic Hebraic understanding of God as a God of history. Simply because the divine nature is essentially one of personal purpose, the ultimate character of God must be expressed by the final state of history. What *is* ultimately real *will be* ultimately realized. Whereas to the Greek the essential was what is true *timelessly,* to the Hebrew it was what still holds true *at the end of time.* For the Bible, the eternal is that which abides, which outstays everything else. To view the world *sub specie aeternitatis* is to view it *sub specie finis.* For the end, rather than the non-historical, is what expresses the complete and perfect will of God.[1] Consequently, to see in history the hand of the eternal is to see in history the mark of the *eschaton.* For the prophetic outlook, every event which genuinely reveals and embodies the will of God must thereby prefigure that ' consummation ' which ' the Lord, the Lord of hosts, shall make in the midst of the whole earth' (Is. 10.23).

This accounts for the fact that the prophets found it necessary to see the impending events of their time through the often lurid light of eschatological expectation. It was the Hebraic manner of expressing the conviction that God

[1] Karl Heim makes the same point when he says: ' So long as God is for us only the terminus of a vertical line which leads directly upwards from every point of history, so long as the horizontal line on which we move loses itself in either direction in the mists of endless duration to which we can put no term, then we are not yet out of the realm of atheism ' (*Jesus der Welt-vollender*, p. 156).

47

was in these events. It also explains why predictions of plain historical occurrences, like battles and sieges and famines, alternate so bewilderingly with the most extravagant imagery of supernatural catastrophe. The traditional 'signs of the end' might include cosmic calamities beside which an atomic explosion would pale into insignificance; but no writer seems to have been conscious of any incongruity in fusing and interlarding them with happenings of purely passing and local significance. It was simply the recognized method of asserting that they were *not* of purely passing and local significance; they were acts of God embodying a purpose whose eternal quality was evinced by the nature and certainty of its end. Every genuine revelation of divine judgment and divine mercy reflected, and must be pictured as reflecting, on the sky of human history the fire and lightning of that great Day of the Lord ready to be revealed in the last time.

Moreover, just as every historical event which embodied the eternal must in a measure be eschatological, so, conversely, the last divine event, the *eschaton*, must in some sense be historical. This, again, was a necessary conclusion from belief in a God who was a God of history. To the Hebrew mind, the expression of the most real was not timeless essence, but historical event. What was most unshakably true about God must prove itself not to mystical contemplation but to historical verification. What God is, is what in history he asserts himself to be. Consequently, the ultimate truth about God is necessarily the final event in history. If the last word about God is that he is mercy and loving-kindness, then this must express itself for a Jeremiah or a Second Isaiah in the assurance of a new covenant and a recreated universe as the last word about history. And again here we notice, as it were from the other side, the same intermingling of historical prediction and supernatural imagery. The final consummation cannot but be expressed in the language of myth, and yet, within the myth, the promises assume the form of tangible and material events—

the physical restoration and ingathering of Israel, the provision of wheat and wine and oil, the supply of water in a thirsty land. That this should be true, not only of the grosser imaginings of the apocalyptists,[2] but of the most spiritual visions of the prophets, shows that this materializing tendency occurred in the interests, not of voluptuousness, but of realism. The Hebrew was never afraid of matter. To him it was not the enemy of spirit, but the vehicle and guarantee of its effective reality.

Consequently, in the prophets, we find not only historical expectations drawn as 'types' of the End, but ultimate hopes framed as historical promises. For these promises the events of the day normally afforded little ground : the immediate situation usually justified only the blackest prognostications. Accordingly, the so-called 'hopeful' passages in Hosea and elsewhere have frequently been excised wholesale as interpolations. It is probable that in such matter there may well be later additions, but to discard the prophecies simply because they are out of keeping with the historical prospects is to misunderstand the whole ground of prophetic confidence. Such deliverances are not primarily guesses about the turn of future events : the prophets were not political weather-cocks. They are statements, rather, of conviction about the eternal nature of a God whose last word *could* not be one of destruction. They represent, as has often been said, insight rather than foresight.

But the significant thing is that this insight had to express itself in the form of that peculiarly Hebraic virtue, *hope*. The Jew was not content, as the Greek would have been, to comfort himself that in the midst of temporal disaster the eternal, timeless realities of God stood unshaken. That con-

---

[2] Typically, for instance, in Ethiopic Enoch, 10.17 ff., where in the Messianic kingdom the righteous will beget a thousand children; of all the seed that is sown each measure will bear ten thousand grains; and each vine will have ten thousand branches, and each branch ten thousand twigs, and each twig ten thousand clusters, and each cluster ten thousand grapes, and each grape yield twenty-five measures of wine!

viction must express itself for him in the assurance of an
actual deliverance in a historical future. Though the message
of the prophets did not derive from history, it inevitably
formulated itself in terms of history. For they knew no
other way of saying that the truths of God were realities
than to assert that ultimately they must be realized. And
as a test of their veracity they were consequently prepared
to welcome the verdict of history. If insights failed to
validate themselves in events, then they could not be
genuine. It was not the false philosopher or the false mystic
who was the type of deception in Israel, but the false
prophet.

The shift of key from prophecy to apocalyptic did nothing
essentially to disturb this fundamental assumption of a final
equation between truth and history, though it was to have far-
reaching consequences for its interpretation and ultimately
for its validity.

The writers of the apocalypses continued to share the
axiomatic Hebraic belief that God was what he asserted
himself to be, and that meant what *in the end* he asserted himself to be. Consequently, the Day of the Lord, with its
establishment of the undisputed sovereignty of God over his
world, remained for them the all-controlling category of
interpretation. Where they differed was not in questioning
the vindication of reality in event, but in doubting whether
such an event could adequately be represented as merely
historical. The justification of God came to be expected
in a supra-mundane rather than a purely earthly kingdom.
The distinction must not be exaggerated. The renovated earth
of prophetic vision was bathed in ' a light that never was on sea
or land,' and the necessity for a new heaven and a new
earth, which dominated the later apocalypses, is found in Is.
65.17. Moreover, apocalyptic expectation in one of its
most persistent forms supposed that, prior to the final triumph
of God, there would be established a Messianic kingdom,
albeit a temporary one, on this earth.[3] Nevertheless, the shift
of key is unmistakable. The end of history is no longer

[3] The imagery of the Son of man coming on the clouds of

regarded simply as an event within history: its *telos* has become trans-historical.

There were various reasons of an immediate nature for this change, of which the most important were the apparently hopeless deterioration of the national fortunes and the growing influence of Greek thought with its depreciation of the significance of history. But the ultimate reason, which is easily obscured, is a change in the popular understanding of God, deriving originally from the prophets themselves. If Yahweh were really the transcendent Lord of the universe, before whom the nations of the world were as a drop in a bucket, then it was incredible that he could set up his rule in the Jerusalem that now is. The advent of God— the idea that 'the Lord shall suddenly come to his temple' —is increasingly replaced by the advent of a vice-regent Messiah, while the final and eternal expression of the divine sovereignty is located in the supra-historical order. More- over, the moral as well as the metaphysical transcendence of God as taught by the prophets necessarily pointed in the same direction. If the Lord were of purer eyes than to behold iniquity, nothing short of another Flood could make this earth a fit habitation for the Kingdom of God. The Jew of the first and second centuries B.C. looked out upon a world of power-politics and competing selfishnesses in which the abomination of desolation seemed to be set securely in the centre of God's earth. Over everything was the hand of corruption and force. If God was to be vindicated in a universe of righteousness and love, then surely such a universe could not be this one.

The great contribution of the apocalyptists was to formulate an understanding of history as a process with an end and a meaning which it could not itself embody, *without* surrend- ering the Hebraic insistence that it *had* an end and a meaning. They preserved the eschatological outlook unshaken against

heaven and the, to us, fantastic representation of Christians being 'caught up in the clouds, to meet the Lord in the air' (1 Thess. 4.17) may be taken as spatial symbolism of the truth that God's kingdom must, as it were, be something half-way between heaven and earth.

any Hellenic temptation to write off history as cyclical and abandon hope in the future for knowledge of the timeless.

But while the apocalyptists developed the prophetic teaching in this direction to fulfil it, they expounded it in another in a manner whose eventual result was, if not to destroy it, at any rate to bring it into disrepute.

The prophetic movement rested, as we have seen, on the assumption that there exists a necessary correspondence between ultimate verity and final fact. This conviction prompted the peculiarly Hebraic criterion for assessing truth : ' And if thou say in thine heart, How shall we know the word which the Lord hath spoken? When a prophet speaketh in the name of the Lord, if the thing follow not, nor come to pass, that is the thing which the Lord hath not spoken : the prophet hath spoken it presumptuously, thou shalt not be afraid of him ' (Deut. 18.21-2).[4]

But when such a correlation was pressed too literally it ended in casting doubts upon the validity of the whole prophetic interpretation of history. The essential core of the prophetic revelation was an insight into the nature of God, which, because that nature was one of purposive will, must project itself upon the screen of history as foresight. The resulting prophecy was this basic insight translated into terms of the accepted eschatological idiom and the contemporary historical situation. The assessment of the political outlook, which conditioned the form (but not the content) of the prophet's pronouncement, was as subject to fallibility and limitation as that of any other intelligent observer.

But when such a distinction between substance and accident was not observed, when, with the Exile, the Jews were forced back upon the *letter* of the divine Word, the non-fulfilment of specific prophecies caused evident religious

---

[4] The contrary does not follow automatically—namely, that every word fulfilled is a word from the Lord. Deut. 13.1-3 recognizes that false prophets and seers may correctly foretell signs and wonders to lead Israel after other gods. They are regarded as instruments in the hand of Yahweh to prove Israel's fidelity.

difficulty. If one was not to deny the divine source of prophecy, it seemed necessary to show that, despite all appearances, such predictions must yet find fulfilment. It was partly at any rate to meet such a need that apocalyptic developed as it did.

Its early stages can be illustrated in the treatment accorded to the unfulfilled prophecies of Jeremiah and Zephaniah relating to an invasion of Judah from the north, which failed to materialize. Ezekiel, writing from a situation in exile when literal fulfilment was by then impossible, re-edits this prediction in the apocalyptic vision of a great host (Gog) which, in the last days, would attack Jerusalem from the north, and he sees in it the verification of the earlier prophecies (37.17). Thus the Gog-Magog legend was born, which was destined to enter Christian symbolism through the book of the Revelation.

Much more fateful was the non-fulfilment of Jeremiah's prediction of the end of the Exile and the restoration of Israel after seventy years (25.11; 29.10). The baleful influence exerted by this figure 70 can be seen throughout the apocalyptic period, as successive writers seek by various extravagances of mathematical manipulation to show that even now the Kingdom is about to appear according to schedule (e.g., Dan. 9.25-7; Eth. Enoch 39; 90).[5]

Does all this mean that the Hebraic understanding of eschatology had been discredited? Did the apocalyptists expose the fallacy of that correspondence between ultimate truth and final fact demanded by the prophets, or did they misunderstand it? Can the Christian Faith hold any longer to this basic equation, which is the essence of eschatology? Or would it be wiser, as it has in effect done in recent times, to concentrate on personal immortality in a non-eschatological context? Has it in fact any interest in the *Last* Things in any sense other than the final destiny of the individual?

To answer these questions it is necessary to probe deeper

[5] On this whole subject, see R. H. Charles, A critical history of the doctrine of a future life in Israel, in Judaism, and in Christianity, pp. 168-73.

into the Hebraic understanding of time, and to try to
discover what really was the fundamental thing which the
Biblical writers sought to assert when they spoke so signi-
ficantly of the *last* times and the *end* of the ages.

CHAPTER VI

Kairos and Chronos

In all expressions relating to the end there is a latent ambiguity. The terms 'final' and 'ultimate' carry a double reference. On the one hand, they indicate temporal posterity. The last is that which in a time-sequence comes *after* everything else, the concluding moment after which it is impossible for anything to occur or continue. The position and moment of the end is here defined and determined entirely by its place in a temporal series.

But terms relating to the end stand also for a finality which is not primarily quantitative, but qualitative. The point of reference is fulfilment of purpose rather than simple posterity. The position and moment of the end is defined and determined, not temporarily, but by reference to a state of achievement. The end is that after which nothing further can happen, not because it is physically impossible for duration to continue, but because there is nothing more to happen. The purpose is achieved: anything further would not only not add anything, but, like the thirteenth stroke of a clock, would render meaningless everything that had occurred hitherto. Such an understanding of finality does not exclude the possibility of a supervening state of fruition, as a merely temporal understanding would. Indeed, it presupposes such a state of fruition. For a purpose cut off at the very instant of achievement would not normally be regarded as fulfilled.[1]

[1] Cf. O. C. Quick, *Doctrines of the Creed*, p. 247 (Fontana ed. p. 250): 'The last event or act, which achieves the purpose, is as much a beginning as it is an end. It does not really achieve the end unless it *initiates* a fulfilment; that is why it derives its special importance from what is *beyond* the series of events of which it is the last. A work of art destroyed in the moment of completion could hardly be said to fulfil the artist's aim. A traveller who dropped dead as he set foot on Waverley platform could

It is characteristic of this second way of determining the end that the temporal moment is entirely subordinate to the moral. Because a purpose is essentially something that occurs in time and its fulfilment stands at the close of a series, the end, qualitatively considered, will express itself outwardly as the last point in a temporal succession. But that which determines the end and the date at which it occurs is the moral moment, not the temporal. It is the difference between a book whose scope and size are determined by the fact that it has to be completed and rounded off within a certain length of papyrus roll and a book whose pages stop with the print because there is nothing more to add.

The connection between these two meanings of finality is very close, and any event which completes a purpose can be regarded from either point of view. But which viewpoint is considered the decisive one is highly important, and governs the whole understanding of eschatology.

The distinction we have been making is one that underlies a fundamental difference between two ways of regarding not merely the end but the whole of the time-process. It is a difference which the Biblical writers indicate by their use of the two Greek words for time, *kairos* and *chronos*.[2]

This is not the place to go in any detail into the linguistic usage of the Old and New Testaments in Greek. It will be enough to give the conclusions of such an investigation as they affect the particular problem of eschatology.

The usual word for 'time' in secular Greek is *chronos*.

---

hardly be said to have achieved his purpose in going to Edinburgh. . . . The things then which Christian theology calls "the last" are so called mainly because they fulfil the purpose of this world-process by bringing into existence that state of perfection which the creator originally designed.'

[2] There is by no means a 1:1 correspondence between the two words and the two ways of regarding time. Often the words are virtually interchangeable (as in the familiar phrase 'the times and the seasons'). But, despite the criticism mounted by James Barr in his *Biblical Words for Time* (Chapter II), I am convinced there is here a real and important theological distinction, to which in general the two terms are pointers.

In the Biblical writings, the normal term is *kairos*. It is normal, not merely in the sense that it is more common, but in the sense that it represents the norm or proper standpoint from which time is to be understood. *Kairos* is time considered in relation to personal action, determined by reference to ends to be achieved in it. *Chronos* is time abstracted from such a relation, time, as it were, that ticks on objectively and impersonally, whether anything is happening or not. It is time measured by the chronometer not by purpose, momentary rather than momentous.

The fundamental assertion made about time by the Bible is that it is God's time. He is over it as its Lord. The times and the seasons are in the Father's own power (Acts 1.7): they are *kairos idioi* (1 Tim. 2.6; 6.15; Titus 1.3), 'his own' to dispose. Time, therefore, is a function of the divine purpose and only truly to be assessed by reference to it. What we call history is not merely neutral succession of events but his story, God's *kairoi*—moments of opportunity appointed by him and decisive for men, in which his design is either advanced or retarded. All things and events are subordinate to this single overarching purpose. There is no occurrence which may not and must not be interpreted by it: 'To every matter there is a time (*kairos*) and a judgment (*krisis*)' (Eccles. 8.6, R.V. marg.). And each particular moment of judgment makes its contribution towards the supreme consummation toward which all is working—the final *kairos* which is also the final *krisis*.

This is the real truth about time. But it is possible to abstract from the personal purpose and regard history simply as chronology or chronicle. *Chronos* is time removed from reference to God and regarded as self-determining. It is time given an autonomy which it does not by right possess. Like other idols it is regarded by the Biblical writers as ineffectual: time in itself, as opposed to God, determines nothing, except in so far as man allows himself to become its slave and so loses the freedom and a purchase over events which are his when he responds to them as *kairos*. The error comes in regarding time as having an existence and movement of its own, as though in itself it decided anything. This reversal of its true understanding leads men to reckon that events can be predicted at a certain date, as though time (*chronos*) and not God were the determining factor in when they should occur. This is the essence of determinism— that something will happen at a given moment whatever is done in the interval. It is the abandonment of belief that what decides when things shall occur is a purpose which respects and takes into account the response of human freedom. For if human reaction is to make a genuine difference, then it is clearly something that can retard or hasten the accomplishment of the event in question. A thing can only be predicted with certainty to take place at a given moment if it is the clock (*chronos*) and not maturity of purpose (*kairos*) that decides when that moment shall be.

It is a transition from an understanding of time as *kairos* to an understanding of it as *chronos* that perhaps more than anything else marks the change from the prophetic to the apocalyptic outlook. The transition is, of course, far from complete. The transcendent personal determination of history is still axiomatic for the apocalyptists. But their conception of the actual way in which God directs the historical process is often sub-personal and mechanical. The obsession of later apocalypses with predicting the date of the End, as if that were the heart and test of prophecy, betrays the same assumptions about the determination of events as one finds in the devotees of pyramidology and astrology. It is impersonal because it subordinates the moral moment to the temporal. According to the view of time as *kairos,* the calendar date is both unpredictable and irrelevant. For the End is not determined solely by what remains of the purpose to be achieved. When it will be ripe to occur depends entirely on the personal factors in the situation, divine and human. To these the temporal moment is strictly subordinate.

One could illustrate the difference under discussion by adapting a well-known simile of William James.[3] God,

[3] From 'The Dilemma of Determinism,' in *Essays in Pragmatism,* pp. 62-4.

the master chess-player, takes on the novice, representing man. All moves are open to man and God does not know exactly which his opponent will make. But he knows that, *whatever* the other may do, he will be able to counter it and to win. That is the prophetic position. The apocalyptist goes on to say not simply, 'God will win,' but, 'God will win at move 30.' And between these two is all the difference between freedom and determinism. In the one *kairos* determines *chronos*, in the other *chronos* determines *kairos*. Whenever, indeed, the prophets were betrayed in effect into saying, 'God will win at move 30' (e.g., Jeremiah's seventy years), they were, like the apocalyptists after them, invariably wrong. This in itself should indicate the falsity of this measure for reckoning God's workings. It was not in fact an estimate derived from the peculiarly Hebraic experience of God, but a yard-stick imported from the Chaldeans and astrologers.

In the New Testament there are plenty of traces of the apocalyptic attitude to time, which had gained a great hold on popular thought. But, even in the book of the Revelation, it does not appear in the thorough-going form which involves itself in the calculation of dates. The most obvious sign of its influence is in the conviction, doomed to frustration, of an *early* return of the Messiah. To this question we shall come back in a moment.

Meanwhile, it is clear that in the pages of the New Testament as a whole the prophetic outlook is dominant. One has only to study the use of *kairos* in the concordance to be convinced of that. The distinctive Hebraic outlook can be illustrated from a passage in what is probably the last book of the New Testament to be written, 2 Peter, which in its imagery is much influenced by apocalyptic. It represents a deliberate attempt to correct an expectation based on a misunderstanding of time as *chronos*. 'Forget not this one thing, beloved, that one day is with the Lord as a thousand years, and a thousand years as one day. The Lord is not slack concerning his promise, as some count slackness; but is long-suffering to you-ward, not wishing that any should perish, but that all should come to repentance' (2 Pet. 3.8-9).

This does not mean, as Hellenic theology interpreted it, that time intervals are unreal to God, who is outside time altogether. It means that what determines the moment of consummation has nothing to do with the almanack. Whether it takes a thousand years or one day is all the same to God. For the true measure of time is his *kairos* and not man's *chronos*. Delay indicates, not that he is behind the clock (as if that were what determined the tempo of history), but the quality of his purpose—namely, the fact that the moment of closure is entirely subordinate to the yearning and patience of a love treating with persons.

How Jesus himself viewed the matter will perhaps never be settled: there is too much secondary material in the Gospel apocalypses to allow any dogmatic assertion.[4] It is, however, worth pausing to consider one saying (which, from its limitation of the power of the Son, has every probability of being genuine), because it shows that the issue cannot be decided on superficial exegesis. The saying is that recorded in Mark 13.32: ' Of that hour or that day knoweth no one, not even the angels in heaven, neither the Son, but the Father.' At first sight this might seem to imply that there is a map of the future, chronologically determined, which is known beforehand to God. But what the Father knows is not the *chronos* but the *kairos*. The ' hour ' and the ' day ' for New Testament usage are concepts essentially to be defined in terms of *kairos*, of time in relation to purpose: they indicate not neutral divisions of the calendar, but moments for action or decision.[5] And to say that the Father knows the final *kairos* is not to say that he knows the date of the end. (Prescience *of this kind*, which would involve

4 I have explored this question in detail in my book *Jesus and His Coming*.

5 Cf., out of many instances, Luke 22.53: ' But this is your hour, and the power of darkness'; Mark 14.35: 'He . . . prayed that, if it were possible, the hour might pass away from him'; John 13.1: ' Jesus, knowing that his hour was come . . .'; Rev. 3.10: ' I will also keep thee from the hour of trial, that hour which is to come upon the whole world '; Luke 17.24: ' So shall

'determinism and denial of human freedom, is never predicated of God by the Biblical writers when they are true to the characteristically Hebraic outlook.) For the chronological moment of the end is utterly irrelevant for determining the completion of God's purpose. It is of interest only to the curious, to the spectators of history. 'Knowing the hour' is not knowing something that can be calculated in terms of years and months (as certain of the apocalyptists thought, and certain of their modern disciples still think, only to be confounded time and time again by the evidence of history's continuance). It is the knowledge of something that can be assessed solely in terms of the purposes yet to be achieved. It is knowledge limited to the Father because he alone can determine the moment when his design has reached its maturity: in his omniscience he declares the final *kairos*. Creatures, as beings 'in time,' whose own the *kairoi* are not, cannot know this, because it is not they who determine it. And the Son, as man, is equally subject to this limitation. But the Father is the one in whose power the times and the seasons are. He knows the end; but it as Lord of the *kairoi* and not as Spectator of the *chronoi*.

The difference between these two ways of determining the End may perhaps be clarified further by an illustration from the British (in contrast with the American) political system. The date of a general election as an administration nears the term of its mandate is a matter for decision by the Government alone. No one outside the confidence of the

---

the Son of man be in his day'; 2 Cor. 6.2: 'Behold now is the acceptable time (*kairos*), now is the day of salvation'; Heb. 4.7: 'He again defineth a certain day, saying in David, after so long a time (*chronos*): To-day . . . if ye shall hear his voice, harden not your hearts.' In this last instance, the contrast comes out clearly between *kairos*, time in intimate relation to personal action and decision, and *chronos*, time out of such relation, and therefore meaningless duration, delay. The phrase in Rev. 10.6, 'there shall be time (*chronos*) no longer,' which has been the basis of much theologizing about the supersession of time in eternity, means 'There shall be no more delay' (R.V. marg., R.S.V., and N.E.B.).

Cabinet can know it. But the dissolution is fixed by the Prime Minister, not for some arbitrary date that could be calculated in advance by the Opposition if it discovered the formula, but for the moment when he and his advisers judge the time most opportune for an appeal to the country. This will arise either sooner or later, according to all kinds of contingencies that may occur in the interval. The fixing of the election-date depends on a personal purpose which takes them all into account. Of course, in this instance there is also an element of *chronos*-determination : Parliament must by law be dissolved before five years are up, however untimely this may be for the Government. But the contrast between the two types of determination, personal and mechanical, is clear enough.

In the light of all this, let us now turn to that very considerable body of evidence in the New Testament which, though it declines to place any date upon the coming of the End and the return of Christ, undoubtedly regards it as *temporally* extremely near.

There are two considerations to bear in mind. First, it was an expectation that was not fulfilled. Unless the whole Hebraic equation between truth and fact is false, this in itself would suggest that it rested upon a misapprehension. But the second consideration is more important. It is that the Church, unlike scores of millenarian movements before and since, survived the non-fulfilment of this expectation, and survived it, apparently, with remarkable ease. This would indicate; either that the hope of a Second Advent in any form was inessential to its preaching, or that the note of *temporal* immediacy was a misunderstanding of an urgency in itself independent of it.

Now, it is impossible to cut the expectation of the Parousia entirely out of New Testament Christianity. Nor, in fact, historically, was the storm weathered by treating the doctrine of the Second Coming as ballast. 'He shall come again to judge the quick and the dead' stands securely in the Church's creeds.

This leaves the second possibility—namely, that the idea of temporal immediacy rested, and was discovered to rest, on a misapprehension of another truth. In the light of the distinction drawn in this chapter, one may see how this in fact was the case. It is possible to show how the prevailing popular expectation of an imminent Advent rested upon a misinterpretation, in terms of a *chronos*-outlook, of a message whose essential truth was bound up with the genuinely Hebraic attitude to time as *kairos*. Consequently, when the hope of an early return was disappointed, the adjustment could be made without surrendering anything essential to the apostolic preaching.

Consider, first, a phrase which sums up the whole of the primitive expectancy: ' The time is short '—*ho kairos sunestalmenos estin* (1 Cor. 7.29). In its context it is clear that Paul understands this in terms of temporal brevity. But in themselves the words do not necessarily imply an immediate end of the world. *Sunestalmenos*, as the R.V. indicates, means ' shortened ' or, better, ' narrowed down.' And what is thus contracted is not *chronos*, duration, but *kairos*, the time for decision. In other words, the time for response and commitment is cut down; there is an inescapable urgency about the decision to be made (cf. the derivation of our own word ' decisive ' from the Latin *decaedo*, cut down).

To be brought home effectively to men's consciences such moral urgency has necessarily, perhaps, to be *expressed* as temporal urgency, decisiveness of *kairos* translated into immediacy of *chronos*. The element of decisiveness, for instance, in a football match is expressed by a definite time-limit. If there never came a moment when the whistle would blow and one side would have won or lost, all seriousness or interest would vanish from the game. And yet it remains true that the moral responsibility of playing as hard as one can is not derived from the temporal urgency. A matter is not really made morally more urgent by the fact that one has only a short while in which to make up one's mind about it. Such urgency is derived from the intrinsic nature of the situation and cannot be increased or decreased by time, any more than it can be by space.[6]

If this is true, then it can be seen that the note of temporal imminence, struck so constantly in the New Testament, is only an external way of expressing the essential element in Christian eschatology, which is that of moral urgency. The writers themselves may perhaps often have confused the substance and the form, and written as though it were *chronos* that determined *kairos* and not *vice versa*. But their essential message was one of *kairos* and not *chronos*, and this meant that it could stand even if it were no longer interpreted as involving an immediate end. Consequently, the Church was able to retain the New Testament gospel that Christians were living in the last days without being perplexed unto despair by the fact that 'the last days should last so long.'[7] If the true Biblical understanding of time is grasped, then the Advent Epistle is equally true for all generations and all times: 'Love thy neighbour as thyself ... And this, knowing the season (*kairos*) that now it is high time for you to awake out of sleep: for now is salvation nearer to us than when we first believed. The night

[6] There is indeed another strand in the Gospel teaching which bears out the fact that shortness of chronos is not the automatic expression of urgency of *kairos*. It stresses urgency of faithful response *in spite of* temporal delay. The temptation for the servant of Christ will be to relax moral effort and to say: 'My Lord delayeth his coming, (Luke 12.45). It is true that there is here propounded the alternative sanction of unexpectedness to keep men up to the mark (cf. Pet. 3.8-10). This is but another way of translating into non-moral terms the searchingness of the moral demand. But it does indicate that it was recognized that there might not be a 1:1 correspondence between *kairos* and *chronos*. In the similar parable of the Vineyard, it is said (Luke 20.9) that the owner went away into another country *chronous hikanous*—'for an indefinite period' or 'for a sufficient time.' Its duration (*chronos*) was entirely subordinate to his purpose; it determined nothing, and is therefore treated freely. It does not affect the urgency of the issue upon which the husbandmen had to decide.

[7] A. R. Vidler, *Christ's Strange Work*, p. 30.

is far spent, and the day is at hand: let us therefore cast off the works of darkness, and let us put on the armour of light' (Rom. 13.9-12). The moral urgency is expressed in the temporal, not derived from it.

A position has now been reached in which it is possible to return some answer to the questions raised at the close of the previous chapter. We noted how the apocalyptists, while deepening the understanding of the *eschaton* by insisting that it could not be simply this-worldly, also brought into discredit the prophetic principle, on which the whole of eschatology rests, of a necessary correspondence between ultimate truth and final event. By lapsing from the prophetic understanding of time as *kairos*, they turned history into a process whose developments were governed by the calendar, or, rather, were determined by a divine Planner whose programme could be calculated from the calendar.[8] Now between the ultimate nature of God and the end of history calculated by this measure there could not be—and in fact there was not—any necessary correspondence. But that does not in itself impugn the fundamental Hebraic insight of the validity of *eschatology*, viz., that the truest is what is true in the end, that the ultimate must be the final.

What the investigation of *kairos* and *chronos* has shown is that there is not necessarily a simple correspondence between temporal and moral finality. *To claim that there is is always to exalt temporal finality above the moral as the determining factor.* It is to reverse the eschatological equation: to say that the final in time is the ultimate in significance, rather than that the ultimate in significance is the final in time. Now for such reversal there are no valid grounds. The last event in a temporal series, *just because it is the last*, has no more importance than any other event: it can claim no

[8] It is interesting to observe the change which has passed over the word *kairos* in Daniel's use of such phrases as 'a time, and times, and half a time' (i.e., $3\frac{1}{2}$ years). *Kairos* is no longer a moment for challenge and decision, whose length is determined solely by purpose, but a fixed chronological period whose bounds are set in advance.

ultimacy for the purposes of interpretation. In a chess match, for instance, the final move may in fact be move thirty; but it has not *thereby* any more decisive significance for the issue of the game than moves twenty-nine, twenty-eight, or sixteen. Though it concludes the game, it may by comparison with earlier moves be quite inconclusive. To say, however, as in effect the apocalyptists did, that 'God will win at move thirty' is to invest this move with a decisive and teleological significance which merely by reason of its temporal finality it cannot possess. It is no longer simply that which ends the series, but that which forecloses it: by the time move thirty is reached, the match will have been won. It has become what determines the issue and decides when the purpose is achieved.

Or perhaps one can fix the point by yet another illustration. A man may die at 8 a.m. on September 15th, or a man may have to die at 8 a.m. on September 15th. In the first case, the hour is quite unimportant: when the span of his life draws to its close, when his time (*kairos*) comes, the clock simply registers it—the fact that 8 a.m. is his last temporal moment determines nothing. In the second case, however, the last moment, as the hands move up to eight o'clock becomes all-decisive: it determines the *kairos*, and, so far from having no significance in itself, its effect, as Dr. Johnson once remarked, is to 'concentrate the mind wonderfully.'

To assert with the apocalyptists that there is a necessary correspondence between *kairos* and *chronos* is always to say the world must die on a certain date, and to give to *chronos* the determination of *kairos*. But if one abandons this perversion of the prophetic truth, the eschatological principle still stands—the ultimate truth will be final fact. But the moment of temporal finality loses any *peculiar* significance. The temporal end (or *finis*) will certainly reflect and embody the moment of ultimate significance (as the last move of a chess match translates into finality the move that really won), but it will not necessarily itself be the *eschaton*, the finalizing *kairos*, the moral *telos*. That may occur anywhere in the process. The eschatological character of this moment is not governed by its temporal finality.

This is an insight which, as will become clear in the next chapter, is of decisive importance for the Christian understanding of the Last Things.

CHAPTER VII

The End of the Times

The New Testament message is that Jesus is the final revelation of the divine nature, the last word of God and about God. This means that he is also viewed automatically as the last word about history: in him 'the time is fulfilled' (Mark 1.15). 'Now once at the end [R.V. marg., consummation] of the age hath he been manifested' (Heb. 9.26). The supreme disclosure of God's nature cannot come at any time; it cannot come, as a pagan theophany might, against the backcloth of history which has nothing to do with it and which it leaves unaffected. For the God of the Incarnation is the God of history. He can speak finally about himself only as he speaks finally about the world-process. With the completion of Christ's work, *tetelestai*, 'it is finished' (John 19.30): the *telos* of history is finally revealed.

This is otherwise expressed in the New Testament by the paradoxical affirmation that the *eschaton* has arrived.[1] The last times have begun, the powers of the age to come have broken in upon the present order. In the person and work of Christ the kingly rule of God is already a present reality: 'If I by the finger of God cast out devils, then is the kingdom of God come upon you' (Luke 11.20). That beyond which nothing can happen has already happened. Such is the message that runs through the whole of the New

[1] *To eschaton* (neuter) is not actually a New Testament phrase. Loyalty to the Christocentric nature of all New Testament theology would require us to speak always of *ho eschatos*—not the last Thing, but the last Man. So in Rev. 1.17; 2.8; 22.13, Christ is essentially *ho protos kai ho eschatos*, the first and the last. In 1 Cor. 15.45 he is *ho eschatos Adam*, 'the eschatological man.' The Jesus of history is 'the Son of man on earth' (Mark 2.10), the eschatological figure of the apocalypses exercising his functions of forgiveness and judgment 'before the time,' within this present world-order.

68

Testament, Gospels, Acts, and Epistles.[2] Though his contrast between St. Paul and the rest of the early Church has clearly been shown to be false, Schweitzer's metaphor still makes the point with arresting force: 'While other believers held that the finger of the world-clock was touching on the beginning of the coming hour and were waiting for the stroke which should announce this, Paul told them that it had already passed beyond the point, and that they had

[2] It is perhaps worth adding that the gospel of 'realized' (or, as I would prefer to put it, 'inaugurated') eschatology is attested by many passages in the New Testament which to the modern ear have no eschatological ring at all. For instance, the very gift of the Spirit as a corporate possession of Body, available not merely, as under the Old Covenant, to outstanding individuals, prophets, and kings, but to every member of the People of God down to slaves and scullions, was itself seen as sure evidence that 'the last days' had come (Acts 2.17-18). The fantastic wish that 'all the Lord's people were prophets, that the Lord would put his spirit upon them' (Num. 11.29) had in these latter days become a reality. All that the New Testament has to say of life in the *koinonia*, or common ownership, of Holy Spirit, is direct assertion that the New Age of the Kingdom has already begun in this world. When St. Paul is speaking of 'the fruits of the Spirit' he is talking about eschatology. If evidence such as this be taken into account, the passages relating to a future coming can be seen to occupy a comparatively minor place in the eschatological message of the early Church. It may be noted, for instance, when estimating the relative emphasis laid on the two elements, that St. Paul, like Jesus, never derives any *moral principle* from the belief in the Second Advent: the whole quality of the Christian life is based directly upon the fact that Christians *have already been* translated into a new order of existence: 'If then ye were raised together with Christ, seek the things that are above. . . . For ye died and your life is hid with Christ in God' (Col. 3.1-3); 'Ye are not in the flesh, but in the spirit, if so be that the Spirit of God dwelleth in you. . . . So then, brethren, we are debtors, not to the flesh, to live after the flesh' (Rom. 8.9, 12). The future hope is used simply to underline the urgency (e.g., Rom. 13.11-12), never to formulate the principle. It is permitted on occasion to modify the details of application (1 Cor. 7.29), but even in this respect St. Paul found it necessary to correct those who were allowing their conduct to be distorted by undue emphasis upon an immediate Parousia (1 Thess. 4.11).

failed to hear the striking of the hour, which in fact struck at the Resurrection of Jesus.'[3]

That beyond which nothing can happen had already happened. This goes to explain the prevailing certainty among the New Testament writers that time must shortly come to an end. The decisive move had been played. The opposition *must* resign: it had no *right* to continue. Though, as we have seen, there is no necessity that finality of purpose should automatically be marked by temporal cessation, such is the inevitable form of expression by which this finality is asserted. The idea of the Second Advent stands in the New Testament for the conviction that if the events of the Incarnation have the eschatological character asserted of them, then history *must* come to a close. And by the process already discussed, ' the proposition " A is involved in B " (by the logic of the moral and spiritual order) becomes " A will follow immediately upon B ".'[4]

But the idea of the Second Advent represents also the inescapable conviction that the end of God's purpose, however clearly embodied in the Incarnation, has *not yet* come in the most final sense possible. And that is evidenced, not merely in the outward fact that the temporal process continues, but in the more fundamental fact that God and his will are obviously not all in all. In order to understand the finality of the events of the Incarnation, in order to see them as *eschatological* at all, it becomes necessary to view them as the first half of a single process that will be completed in the future. It becomes necessary, to borrow a metaphor used by both Barth and Heim, to assume the thunder in order to interpret the lightning. It is the certainty of the sequel which seals the events of the Incarnation as eschatological.

It is important to see this motive for the formulation and retention of the belief in a Second Advent. It explains, for instance, why an element of ' futurist eschatology' remains even in those strands of the New Testament, such

[3] *The Mysticism of Paul the Apostle*, p. 99.
[4] C.H. Dodd, *The Parables of the Kingdom*, p. 71; Fontana ed. p. 55.

as the Fourth Gospel, where the stress is laid upon the fact of living already in the New Age and the Last Judgment. In St. John, 'the last day' as a future occurrence never entirely disappears (John 6.39-40, 44, 54; 12.48), and it is strongly present in the Johannine Epistles. The offer of eternal life, now, in Jesus Christ is, to be sure, made to rest firmly upon the eschatological character of the *first* Advent. The themes of the Synoptic Gospels of the coming of the kingdom of God in power, the exaltation of the Son of man to his throne of glory, and his return in judgment and great might, are tied securely to the historical events of Good Friday, Easter Day, and Whitsunday. The so-called 'second' Coming (not in fact a New Testament phrase) is viewed as the return of the risen Christ in the power of the Spirit.[5] But it is precisely to insist on the ultimate, eschatological character of these 'first' events—and not to detract from it—that the limiting concept of the 'last day' is retained.

The function of this imagery is to indicate in unmistakable idiom the *finality* of the processes of life and death, salvation and judgment, set in motion by the events of the Incarnation. The world-judgment is already in action. Outwardly it does not look like it. It appears, as it appeared to a writer of the second century, that 'all things continue as they were from the beginning of the creation' (2 Pet. 3.4). So, into the main picture the New Testament writers introduce an inset—a glimpse of 'that day' when the Lord would be all in all and his will should have free course and be glorified. This inset was not put there simply by way of antithesis to the main scene, as though to suggest

[5] Cf. the deliberate reinterpretation in the Last Discourses of the eschatological ideas like the 'little while' and the 'coming' in 'that day' to 'convict the world.' These discourses occupy the same place prior to the Passion narrative as the apocalyptic discourses do in the Synoptists. In the Johannine writings 'the day of the Son of man' becomes 'the hour . . . that the Son of man should be glorified' (John 12.23), and the 'signs of the end' the 'marks' of the New Age within the Church—'the Spirit and the water and the blood' (1 John 5.6-8; cf. John 7.38-9; 19.34). See the fuller treatment of Johannine eschatology in *Jesus and His Coming*, Chapter VIII.

that the present situation was merely penultimate and would be superseded one day by another, final state. It was there, as it were, as the key to the proper understanding of the present. It is the great *clarification* (*apocalypsis*) of the truths that now are, so that every eye may see. ' The Parousia removes the hiddenness of the reality of Easter for history.'[6] At the Resurrection the winning move was played. Thenceforward the issue of the game could not be in doubt. The picture of the end-time is a representation of the check-mate which *must* follow because in fact it is already contained in the decisive move.

The limiting idea of the ' last day' serves in the Fourth Gospel a purpose somewhat analogous to that of the Trans-figuration in the Synoptists. The Transfiguration narrative is not intended to throw into doubt the divinity of the humili-ated Christ by contrast with an ultimate, exalted state. On the contrary, it is a turning back of the corner of the veil to reveal the essential, the eschatological, glory which now is, and which constitutes the real truth about the present humiliation. Both this and the ' last day ' are ideal pictures to authenticate, rather than detract from, the finality of the immediate situation.

But, again, though this finality is stressed in various ways and in various degrees by the whole witness of the New Testament, it is also never forgotten that the present situa-tion is one in which the rule of God has not yet completely superseded the powers which control this age. Their death-warrant is signed, they are in the process of annihilation (1 Cor. 2.6), but their force is still active. The eclipse of the old order is yet only partial, but the sun has begun to move across its disc. Christians, as those who belong to the new and yet who still inhabit the old, live, as it were, in the area of intersection: they are those upon whom the ' ends of the ages' have overlapped (the probable force of *katenteken* in 1 Cor. 10.11).

Consequently, the Christian era and the Christian life are viewed in the New Testament as set between two poles,

[6] P. Althaus, *Die letzten Dinge,* 4e Aufl. p. 244.

between the fact that the end has come and the fact that
the end is yet to be. Every great New Testament phrase
reflects this double reference: the kingdom of God, eternal
life, salvation, justification, sanctification, perfection, even
glorification, are all spoken of as being at one and the
same time present possessions based on past fact and objects
of full attainment only in the future. Sunday is at once a
remembrance of the first Lord's day and a foretaste of the
last: it symbolizes the eschatological time between the Resurrection and the Parousia. The Eucharist, the pattern-action
of the whole Christian life, also takes place between these
two poles, between the Last Supper and the Great Supper.
It proclaims the Lord's death as an act of re-presentation
and it celebrates in anticipation the banquet of the Messiah
'till he comes.' It is 'as true a subsistence of those things
past which we believe, as it is of those things yet to come
which we hope for.'[7] The celebrating community, as 'the
Lord's remembrancer,' sets forth the real presence (Parousia)
both of the First and the Second Coming. As an *anamnesis*
of Calvary and the Resurrection, it is a re-presentation in
the Body of the dying and rising of Christ; as an anticipation
of the Messianic banquet, it is—

> The song of them that triumph,
> The shout of them that feast.[8]

So far in this chapter we have been considering the witness of the New Testament to the meaning of the revelation
of God in Jesus Christ. All the writers speak of it as

[7] Adapted from the Preface by Daniel Brevint to John and
Charles Wesley's *A Selection of Hymns on the Lord's Supper*, p.
8.

[8] Schweitzer (*op. cit.*, p. 252) points out how the Eucharist is
described proleptically by the word *agalliasis*, 'rejoicing' or, better,
'shouting' (Acts 2.46), which is the regular word for the jubila-
tion at the coming of the Kingdom (cf. 1 Pet. 4.13; Jude 24).
It is used in Rev. 19.7 of the wedding banquet of the Messiah:
'Let us be glad and rejoice (*agalliomen*) and give honour to him,
for the marriage of the Lamb is come.'

something which is by its very nature once and for all, unrepeatable, *final*. Yet its very finality in a world that goes on, in a world which is *not yet* the kingdom of God, requires to be asserted by the limiting concept of a Last Day and a Second Advent. If now we are to define further exactly what is meant by this 'limiting concept' we must go back a little and set this New Testament message in the context of what was said in Chapter IV about the nature of revelation and myth.

The basic revelation attested in the New Testament consisted in being confronted, in the person of Jesus and the fellowship of the Spirit, with the *present* reality of the living God. But in Christ the apostolic Church discovered itself laid hold of by someone who filled not only the present but all eternity, who was 'the first and the last, the Alpha and the Omega.' The central truth of the Gospel that God has 'delivered us out of the power of darkness, and translated us into the kingdom of the Son of his love' (Col. 1.13) leads St. Paul on directly to his greatest assertion of its eternal, cosmic implications for the nature of Christ (Col. 1.15-20). And what St. Paul found, so in their different manners did St. John and the others. On the one hand, this Christ authenticates himself not merely as one who became a revelation of the Father at a certain moment of time but as the very Word and Meaning of God from the beginning of the ages. The Church is forced to the affirmation that in him all things were created and that without him was not anything made that was made. And, on the other hand, it recognizes this revelatory act as of such a quality that nothing can supersede it. It is final, it is eschatology: it discloses equally that which must be hereafter. Christ is not only the Alpha but the Omega.

The data of these judgments are given in the present encounter with Christ first in the flesh and then in the Spirit: their *form*, as the consequences are drawn out for the ultimate beginning and end of God's purpose, is myth. The revelation provides no historical information about the

beginning and end of things. Yet the myth is not free speculation. It is a picture designed to bring out the true depths,
the full implication, of the present relationship.

In this book we are concerned only with the implication
of the revelation in Christ for the *Last* Things. Here the
fundamental witness of the apostolic Church was, as we
have seen, that this act of God inaugurated a situation which
was, on the one hand, final, and, on the other, required yet
to be finalized. A picture of the end that was to do justice
to this revelation must include these two elements. This was
achieved by the introduction, into the current Jewish expectation, of the idea of the *return* of the Christ. It was not a new
Christ—there could be nothing new after the final revelation of the Incarnation; on the other hand, the return
stood for the completion of that which was already final.

And yet the purpose of the eschatological myth is not
simply or primarily to draw out implications of what *will be*.
It is first of all a description of what *is*, an inset depicting the
truth of the *present* situation—a situation albeit whose depths
cannot be plumbed wholly in terms of the present. Perhaps
this paradox can most easily be understood by drawing out
the parallel with the Genesis myths of the First Things.[9]

[9] There is a striking parallel between the content of the myths
of the beginning and end, which provides confirmation of the
fact that in form they were both regarded as belonging to the
same genre. The events of the end are depicted as coming to
reverse the events of the beginning. Without going into any
elaborate detail and confining attention to the incidents of Gen.
1-3, one can observe such points as the following. The Fall
narrative ends with the curse upon nature, the promise of toil and
sorrow for man and of birth-pangs for woman, and the expulsion
of Adam and Eve from Eden. The last times begin with terrible
signs of disruption in the natural order, the woes and travails of
the Messianic age, and the casting of the Devil, 'the old Serpent,'
out of heaven. The paradise of Eden is replaced by the Millennium, when, this time the Second Adam dwells with his Bride, the
Church, in a renovated earth; till, finally, all things are handed
back to the Creator from whom they took their origin. The recur-
ring symbol of the tree of life in Genesis and Revelation is an indication of how this parallelism could be worked out almost indefinitely.

For the principles of interpretation in this case have gained a currency and a recognition not yet accorded to the myths of eschatology.

Consider, for instance, the myth of the Fall. The prime motive and intention of the writer is to account for the present, and perennial, condition of man, who in stature and behaviour is at once so like a god and so like a devil. And where as another race or another age might have set out its conclusions in a philosophical system or a scientific treatise, the Hebraic mind tended naturally to express truth in the more concrete form of what to-day would be recognized as the novel or the strip-cartoon. So the author of Gen. 3 makes his sketch. His real interest is not in people who lived thousands of years ago, but in the humanity of his and every age. The abiding greatness of his cartoon, as of any such work of imaginative artistry, lies not in the fact that in it a man can see his ancestors as they were, but that in it he can and must see himself as he is. There, in the domestic life of Everyman, each man is discovered to himself as his own Adam.

Why then does the author place his characters in the first generation rather than in his own? Because he knows the dark mystery of that which he is trying to delineate. Sin is something that may not be understood in terms of one generation alone. Each person and every age knows that he or it is not wholly responsible. All men find themselves born into a historical order in which evil is there before them, dragging them down. Go back into history as far as one may, one can find no generation and no civilization of which this is not true. There seems to be no time when sin was not there anticipating individual choice and decision. It is *not* enough to say that every man is his own Adam, because in this matter no one starts from scratch. The Adam in us is bound up with the historical nexus into which each person is born; and so apparently has it always

---

It is also extended in the New Testament to cover such later myths as those of Babel and the Flood.

been. Consequently, in order to account for the condition of *present* humanity the author of Genesis makes his story tell of the first man and the first woman. It is essential that *in the myth* Adam and Eve shall be historical characters (and not, for instance, legendary heroes or demi-gods who have no place in the historical entail), and of historical characters the first. But it is a total misconception to imagine that the truth of the myth is in any way bound up with their being *actual* figures of history, or that it matters a scrap that as anthropology the whole thing is fanciful.

The same principles must govern consideration of the eschatological myths. The point of reference from which they start is the present. All the elements in the myth are first and foremost descriptions of *present* realities within the life of the New Age. The Second Coming has happened in the return of Christ in the Spirit; the Resurrection of the Body has occurred in the putting on of the new man in the Body of Christ; the Millennium has been inaugurated in the reign of Christ in his Church on earth; the Antichrist is a present reality wherever final refusal meets the Christian preaching; the Messianic Banquet is celebrated whenever the wine is drunk new in the kingdom of God; Satan falls from heaven as each man decides for the Gospel, and in the finished work of Christ the Prince of this world has been judged; the Last Judgment is being wrought out in every moment of choice and decision; Christ is all in all, since all things *have been* reconciled in him.[10]

But in each case these realities cannot, any more than the realities of the kingdom of sin, be understood simply in terms of the present generation. They *are* present realities, but they

[10] The incident at Pentecost of the Apostles speaking in the language of each of the assembled races is probably to be understood as symbolizing, as an accomplished fact, the preaching of the Gospel to all nations, which was one of the signs of the end (Matt. 24.14). At any rate it is at once interpreted by Peter as evidence that these were ' the last days.' This incident is also, of course, to be seen in the context of the reversal of the primal myths referred to above, where it stands for the undoing of Babel.

run out into the ultimate future as the old order runs back
into the primeval past. Just as, to explain the present,
Adam must be depicted in the myth as the first man, so the
New Man from heaven is still 'he that shall come'; the
Resurrection of the Body will not occur till the final day;
for the reign of Christ on earth men must continue to watch
and pray; the Antichrist is a figure belonging to the last
hour; the Messianic Banquet awaits the consummation of the
Kingdom, and for Satan's overthrow the cry still goes up,
'How long?'; the Last Judgment cannot be declared till all
consequences are known, and we see not yet all things
subjected to Christ. The myth, if it is to be true, must,
therefore, present all these elements not simply as present but
also as future.

But, further, in order to do justice to the realities of the
present revelation, it is necessary *in the myth* to represent
these truths not only as future, but as future *events*. As
Adam and the Fall, to explain our situation, must be conceived within the same historical nexus in which we live, so
it is essential that the Parousia, Last Judgment and the rest,
if they are to be relevant for asserting the true, eschatological
character of this present age, shall be depicted as historical
events. Thus every *kairos* and every *krisis* in the present order
(for instance, the fall of Jerusalem) can be seen as eschatological, i.e. as embodying the ultimate judgment on the
world, only if the *eschaton* is conceived as in some way
continuous with the events that prefigure it. *Within the myth*
the Last Things must be viewed as history. It is left to the
form of the imagery employed to make clear that these
ultimate occurrences cannot be conceived as *simply* historical,
but must essentially be trans-historical in nature.[11]

[11] The New Testament never pictures the Parousia, as modern
Liberal and sectarian Christianity has tended to, as another incarnation, Jesus coming again within the sequence and boundaries of
history as we know it. (Such an expectation is typically to be seen
running through Lloyd C. Douglas' popular novel, *The Robe*.) The
return of Christ as judge is always a supernatural event including
a radical transformation, if not a complete supersession, of the
historical scene. There are, it is true, elements in the myth

But it would be an equal misunderstanding to take the picture of the Last Things as *historical prediction* as it is to view Adam and Eve as personages of whom birth-certificates might theoretically be produced. In neither case is the truth of the myth in any way bound up with the belief that its events did literally take place or will do so. Nor is their *temporal* primacy or finality the clue to their real import. The incidents are not actual occurrences in the past and future, but are representations to interpret present realities in all their primal and eschatological quality. Yet they can do this only if they depict, not abstract truths, but events, and events which run back into the past and out into the future. The myth is to be judged solely for its accuracy in interpreting and illuminating the data, not on the grounds that it provides an account of the probable beginning or end of the world acceptable to the astronomer or biologist. In exactly the same way, as we saw, Freud's use of mythological terms such as Eros and Thanatos is scientific in so far as it helps to interpret and illumine the psychological facts; its truth does not depend on whether these figures can be proved to exist by clinical research.

It will perhaps clarify further the status of the myth of the End if we give yet closer attention to the central element in it—the Day of the Parousia or Second Coming.[12] It is well known to students of the New Testament that there are two very different, and apparently incompatible, manners in which this is expected to occur. One catena of sayings (represented generally, in the Gospels, by Mark) suggests that things will very definitely 'work up' towards the final act of the divine drama. It is bound to be evident to all that matters are reaching a head: 'the signs of the end' will become increasingly apparent in the gathering storm. On

---

(the reign of Christ with his saints in a renovated earth and the resurrection of the body) that stress the necessary truth that what supervenes upon history transfigures rather than destroys it.

[12] See further 'Preaching the Second Coming' in *On Being the Church in the World*, Chapter XIII.

the other hand, there is another tradition (represented, for instance, in the source common to Matthew and Luke) which speaks of the Day of Christ cutting suddenly and unexpectedly across the normal processes of this world. Men and women will be engaged upon their ordinary occupations with no premonition of the end. They will be eating and drinking, marrying and giving in marriage, grinding at the mill and drawing at the well. And then, suddenly, as a lightning flash, the day of the Son of man will be upon them transecting human society, and some will be left and others taken.

Now, clearly, as predictions of a literal historical occurrence these two views are incompatible. It must happen one way *or* the other. But, as elements in the myth, both correspond to factors which require to be met. The day of the Lord is equally something which can only happen as the climax of the world-process *and* something which is the truth about the world-process now and at every time. The Parousia cannot be pictured simply as an event in the future: it takes, as it were, a cross-section of the universe at every age. It is 'the revelation of our Lord Jesus Christ,' the lightning-flash which lays bare to public gaze the naked truth about the world and the situation of every man in it, as at any given moment the individual stands on one side of the line or the other, for Christ or against him. The myth of the Parousia universalizes and clarifies, as in an inset, what must happen, and is already happening, whenever the Christ comes in love and comes in power, wherever are to be traced the signs of his presence and the marks of his cross. Judgment Day is a dramatized, idealized picture of every day. And yet it is not simply every day. The Parousia and the Judgment are not merely cross-sections. They must also be represented, as in the other tradition, as realities which consummate as well as transect the historical process. For the process as a whole has a movement and has a meaning: it 'works up' to a goal.

If this understanding of the *mythical* character of eschatological statement is accepted, it will become clear that the Christian has no more knowledge of or interest in the final

state of this planet than he has of its first. The illusion
that the Bible vouchsafes him such information, if he can
but interpret it aright, requires to be buried as deeply as
similar illusions about the beginning of the world derived from
Genesis.[13] It is perfectly true that in a pre-scientific age no
distinction between myth and history was made—or required.
St. Paul, as presumably Jesus, no doubt thought of the Fall
and the Last Judgment as literal events. But that did not
prevent the Apostle uncovering the real significance of both
myths. Such a failure to distinguish does not seriously distort
the New Testament message. It is enough that the Christian
hope was such that in due course, when and as the necessity
arose, it could be dissociated, first, from the expectation of an
immediate Advent, and then from the belief in a literal
Parousia. Of course, one cannot say that the ' events ' of the
End will *not* literally take place, any more than one can assert
that an Adam and an Eve did *not* live in a garden in Meso-
potamia. The Christian can only declare that he has no
interest in these matters. He is concerned, alike in the
myths of the beginning and of the end, with the present. But,

[13] In regard to the end of the world three things perhaps need
to be said:

(1) The Gospel is not in the least concerned with the ' how '
or ' when.' It is as false to interpret the pictures of the apocalyptists
as answers to these questions as it is to read Gen. 1 as an
historical account of the creation in six days, beginning at 9 a.m.
on October 23rd, 4004 B.C. The Bible is solely concerned with
the ' why,' the ' wherefore,' and the ' whither '—asserting that
the world comes from God, exists for God, and goes to God.
The other questions are for the natural scientist, if he can.

(2) When the New Testament speaks about the end of the
world, it refers not to this earth, nor even to this whole physical
universe, but to this *age* (*aion*). The *aion* is not necessarily the
same as anything that the astrophysicist is talking about. It cannot
be calculated chronologically: it is one of the dispensations of
God's purpose or the divisions of God's time understood as *kairos*.

(3) The New Testament's interest is not primarily in the end
of the world at all, but in the day of the Lord. Because the
kingdom of God in its fullness cannot but transcend every limit
of space and time, the picture of its coming has necessarily to
include the break-up of this world-order. But this disruption
is viewed as quite secondary.

being a Christian, he knows the present for what it is; that is to say, a point too charged with eternity to be understood except by myths which open a door into heaven and focus upon every moment the terrible relevance of the first things and the last, the elemental and the ultimate.

CHAPTER VIII

The End of Man

Hebrew eschatology may be said to have begun when the prophet Amos asked the question: 'Are not ye as the children of the Ethiopians unto me, O children of Israel? saith the Lord. Have not I brought up Israel out of the land of Egypt, and the Philistines from Caphtor, and the Syrians from Kir?' (9.7) For it was the assertion that Yahweh was the God of *all* history and had control of the destiny, not merely of Israel, but of the whole world, that transformed the traditional concept of 'the day of the Lord' from a future promise of local blessing to an ultimate cosmic event, in which Israel's position was one of special responsibility rather than of exclusive privilege (Amos 3.2; 5.18). A doctrine of the end of history became possible when God was seen to have *power over* all history; and men ascribed that power to him only when he was recognized to have a *concern for* all history.

In the same way, an eschatology of the individual became a possibility only at the stage when God was proclaimed as the Lord not only of all the earth but also of the regions under the earth. So long as the dead, in passing to Hades, were cut off from the hand of God and passed out of his presence and power, there could be no promise of eternal life. And, with similar logic, the *power* of God over Sheol was little doubted, directly it was asserted that the nature of his love required a *concern* for those in it. Once he was seen to be the God of Abraham and Isaac and Jacob *as individuals* and not merely as symbols of the People, then their personal destiny could not lie beyond his power.

The final end of man, as of history, is an ultimate inference from the doctrine of God. And this applies to far more than the Hebraic religion. It is a universally valid principle that, as is a man's view of God, so is his estimate

83

of his own end. The one is always a function of the other.

This has been denied. In his beautiful book, *And the Life Everlasting*, to which, as will be obvious, this chapter is deeply indebted, John Baillie summed up his section on the primitive's belief in survival by saying that ' it came, if I may be allowed for the sake of vividness so to express it, *not from the priests but from the psychologists.* It was in no sense a product of ethical idealism or of religious faith and aspiration, but was merely a corollary of the ordinary lay psychology of the time and place.'[1]

Now it is clear that the primitive's prospect of survival was not itself an object of religious hope, let alone the centre of his religious interest; but it is doubtful whether, *at this stage*, it is valid to draw such a distinction between the sacred and secular, religion and science. The question of survival may have been debated in terms which *to-day* would be held to fall within the department of psychology, but the assertion that ' the idea of immortality was at first a purely scientific conception '[2] is surely anachronistic. Moreover, the evidence of the association of burial customs in all ages with religious rite is too strong. That the journey of his soul from this life to the next should be marked by no religious ceremony would have seemed as indecent to the primitive as the prospect to his pagan descendent to-day of being laid to rest by a civil servant. Even where the expectation of survival is doubted, the act of disposal is sensed to require a religious sanction.

It has been noted how a widespread disbelief in an after-life and a general denial of God are both modern and coincident phenomena. *Individuals* may have disputed either without the other, or, more often, given grounds for survival which were independent of religion (at any rate of their professed religion). But, over the whole field, it can be shown, not merely that a belief in God or gods and a belief in an after-life of some sort do in fact go together, but,

[1] *Op. cit.*, pp. 76-1. Italics his.
[2] Quoted by J. Baillie, *op. cit.*, p. 64.

more important, that the *kind* of conception of the hereafter is a direct function of the particular understanding of the divine. To work out this parallelism in brief will help to demonstrate the dependence of the Christian hope on the Christian faith and also serve to distinguish it from expectations commonly confused with it that do in fact rest upon very different theologies.

It is a convenient simplification to classify the different views of the prospect of the individual as doctrines of (1) Survival, (2) Immortality, and (3) Resurrection. Let us consider them in turn.

(1) *Doctrines of Survival*

A theory of survival is the universal primitive conception. Men *go on* after death to another life not essentially different from this. The soul, ghost, or shade becomes dissociated from the physical body and passes over into the region of the dead. The chief characteristic of this future existence is that it is shadowy, pale, bloodless—not immaterial, but unsubstantial. It is, in consequence, seldom viewed with much enthusiasm, let alone with hope. There is *some* evidence, among really primitive tribes, for the idealized version of the poet of 'ampler hunting grounds beyond the night.' The Gilbert Islanders, for instance, are said to believe ' that, as soon as a person dies, his soul or shade ascends into the air and is carried about by the winds whithersoever they may chance to blow. At last it is supposed to arrive at a sort of Elysium called Kainakiki, where the spirits pass their time in feasting, dancing, and whatever occupations were most agreeable to them in their bodily existence.'[3] Or again, rather agreeably, ' the tribes of New Guinea, rendered anaemic by hunger, dream of eating unlimited sago throughout eternity.'[4]

[3] J. G. Frazer, *The Golden Bough*, III, 48 ff; quoted by J. Baillie, *op. cit.*, p. 65.
[4] Quoted by J. Baillie, *op. cit.*, p. 66.

But, in general, conditions in the hereafter are seen simply as an indefinite extension of the present scene. Thus, for the Papuans: 'Life in the other world goes on just like life in this one. Houses are built exactly like houses on earth, and there as here pigs swarm in the streets. Fields are tilled and crops are got in; ghostly men marry ghostly women, who give birth to ghostly children. The same old round of love and hate, of quarrelling and fighting, of battle, murder, and sudden death goes on in the shadowy realm below ground just as in the more solid world above ground.'[5]

This kind of survival is virtually identical with that offered by modern Spiritualism, of which the last could be a description almost without alteration. Parallel pictures of the spirit-world are excerpted by Dom Bede Frost in his *Modern Substitutes for Christianity*.[6] Thus, in Conan Doyle's *Raymond*, Pheneas, speaking through Lady Doyle, announces: 'Your home in the other world is ready for you. . . . There is a round small building in the grounds which is filled with exquisite coloured vibrations into which you go when you want soul's rejuvenation . . . There is an oblong pond round which coloured birds come to drink.' 'Raymond Lodge,' Bede Frost continues, 'tells his father that he lived in a house of brick surrounded by trees and flowers, and that the ground was solid. Claude Bamber assures us that the houses are built by brick-layers and designed by architects. He does not inform us as to whether they are bought from building societies by monthly instalments. But other spirits deny the existence of houses. "We live in open space; our dwelling is immensity . . . Spirits sleep as do mortals. They have no beds, but repose on a velvety kind of grass." . . . "All is peace and beauty," "nothing ever jars, we do not tire." Yet Pheneas complains, "If you do not take an interest in your future home, those who are preparing it lose heart," and "a very high spirit" who died thousands of years ago is heard to exclaim, "I am so tired. Why am I so tired

[5] J. G. Frazer, *op. cit.*, I, 286 ff; quoted by J. Baillie, *op. cit.*, p. 66

[6] Pp. 76-7.

to-night?" and seems to be unhappy, and even cross at
times. It is really very reminiscent of a third-rate boarding-
house or hotel in an inland watering-place or a London
suburb.'

There is no essential difference between modern spiritualism
and primitive animism, except that the modern seems to view
this kind of tedium as *desirable* and news of it as a gospel
from heaven, while his ancestor regarded it at best as
neutral and at worst as hopeless. It is indeed a pathetic
commentary on our age, not merely that it finds the survival
doctrine of the spiritualists a source of hope, but that it
actually makes such a doctrine its religion—an idea entirely
strange to the primitive mind. Moreover, the doctrine
of reincarnation, from whose endless futility the religions
of immortality came as welcome liberators, has now reappeared
as itself a gospel of promise: 'Reincarnation is grace. "It
is grace to be able to go onwards. It is grace to be able to
make good again" (Rittelmeyer) . . . It is no longer redemption *from* reincarnation, but education, redemption
through reincarnation.'[7] Such is the reversal of the considered
verdict of mankind, which has deemed perpetuated human
existence without God to be hell rather than heaven.

Professor Baillie makes the important point that, so far
from the primitive animistic idea of survival *developing* into
a fuller doctrine of immortality, it has in fact always *regressed*
with the advance of civilization. A deeper doctrine came not
as an evolution out of it: it arrived only when the former
had lost its power; or it was preached actually as a message
of deliverance from it. It is unnecessary to repeat the wealth
of evidence which Baillie adduces to illustrate this process
from the history of Greece and Rome, of India and Israel. It
will be enough to enlarge upon the fundamental theological
reasons for it.

The doctrine of survival, or the conception of the future
life as mere continuance, is, in origin, a corollary of
primitive animistic religion. It is well adapted to the level
of this religion, though it never formed the object of religious

[7] P. Althaus, *op. cit.*, pp. 154-5.

hope or the focus of religious interest. Primitive religions all view man's life as bound up with this world and seek to afford him a tolerable harmony with, and control over, its ever-threatening forces of famine, pestilence, and the sword. This kind of religion neither seeks nor offers such purchase over the flux of events or emancipation from the earthly scene as to set men's affections on a life radically discontinuous with the present order. The world of the dead is an extension of this one for those who have passed from the active list; it is a land where 'old soldiers never die; they only fade away.'

This continuation of life on half-pay, adapted as it was to the measure of what existence had to offer, could actually make an appeal to the really primitive, as it apparently does to his sophisticated successor. But the history of the doctrine of survival is a history of its declension alike in popularity and in power. From being faintly pleasurable, it comes to be regarded, first as merely neutral, and later with a sense of hopeless despair. In the grip, too, which it exercised upon the mind and in its importance for conviction and conduct it relapsed steadily.

This declension can be put down to the fact that it had to serve as an eschatology for the individual long after the religions which gave it its rationale ceased to flourish. One of the most significant incidents in the history of religion is the failure of polytheism to produce any corresponding eschatology for the ordinary man. Polytheism supervenes upon primitive animism at a certain level of civilization, as the world which has to be ordered becomes increasingly complex and departmentalized. With the growing purchase of man over events, he comes to invoke powers of culture and order which will afford him a life not tied to the bare immediacies of existence. His gods, besides being still controllers of natural forces (now more clearly distinguished apart), are also conservers of the city, the arts, and the assembly, of all that lifts the spirit of man above that which makes his life 'solitary, poor, nasty, brutish, and short.' Such a religion demands an after-life for the individual which corresponds to this relative emancipation from the conditions of this world. But under polytheism such emancipation was the ultimate destiny only of a tiny minority—the heroes and the demi-gods, for whom alone Elysium was open, and whose ranks were now long closed. A very few might be ' translated ' and snatched from the clutch of death, but *through* the grave and gate of death it offered no hope. For ordinary mortals, the earlier doctrine of survival had to continue to serve. But, as the prospect of such a life increasingly ceased to speak to the needs of civilized man, it lost its attraction and power. When polytheism was itself superseded by pantheism in India and Greece and by monotheism in Israel, the new beliefs in immortality and resurrection came not to fulfil but to deliver from the old.

(2) *Doctrines of Immortality*

Doctrines of this type are the spiritual corollary of the pantheistic religions which supervened upon the bankruptcy of polytheism. Polytheism has never issued by historical evolution in monotheism. It has always resulted in a progressive disintegration of life, morals, and culture. Those whose minds yearned to recover a wholeness of thought and experience, were led both in Greece and India, to return at a more sophisticated level to the undifferentiated unity of primitive religion. They sought satisfaction in a monistic scheme which yet gave reality to the life of the spirit.

In different degrees of intellectualization it is fundamentally the same movement that appears in Plato and Neoplatonism, in the Mystery cults and Western mysticism, and in Hinduism and Buddhism. The starting point of all their doctrines is that the spirit of man is a part of the eternal, universal, divine spirit, and is therefore by nature immortal. There is a ' spark of divinity ' in every man, to be identified with the highest, rational, cultural part of him—the spirit or *nous* or soul. The soul (which is here

quite different from the 'breath' or 'ghost' of a man,
which is what animism meant by the term) is temporally
imprisoned in matter, in the body which is its tomb. At
the dissolution of the flesh, the soul returns intact, 'as
the sparks fly upward,' to be reunited with the Absolute, the
Brahma, the World-Soul.

Because its fundamental theological presupposition is pantheistic (the real, immortal part of a man is a 'bit' of
divinity), this doctrine never really succeeds in establishing
a *personal* immortality. The end of man is always reabsorp-
tion, the overcoming of individuality, which is generally
viewed as evil. When pressed to its limits in the religions
of the East, the doctrine promises a state of bliss for
the individual which is indistinguishable from his annihilation.

In a way that never occurred in primitive religion, the
after-life has here become a centre of religious hope. In
some historical instances, as, for instance, in the Mystery
cults, it formed *the* centre. This stress may indeed partly
represent a further reflection of the point at which polytheism
had most signally failed to meet men's deepest needs. But
everywhere the religious interest was evident. Here was
a religion which preached the essential liberation of the
human spirit from the world of flesh and death, and the
eye of faith and the way of discipline were naturally directed
to that point where at length this consummation would be
enjoyed in its fullness. Even in Plato the religious interest
cannot be concealed. As John Baillie insists,[8] for all the
fact that the arguments of the *Phaedo* are purely philosophical
and have nothing apparently to do with religion, it is not
its *logic* that carries the conviction of the book for us nor
the conviction of the doctrine for Plato himself. What really
moves both us and him is not the force of philosophy;
it is the passion of a *faith* that man is by nature and by
right a citizen not merely of earth but of heaven, that he
has his true conversation in that commonwealth of values
which neither time nor death can touch. The hope of im-

[8] *Op. cit.*, pp. 93, 111-12.

mortality is a corollary of faith, but yet of a faith which knows no personal God. In consequence, it is a hope that can hold out no guarantee of the future as a life of personal communion.

(3) *Doctrines of Resurrection*

Such doctrines—and here we come to the specifically Biblical witness—are the counterpart of a belief in a personal God who is related to persons not as his parts, but as his creatures. Men are not divine nor immortal by nature. For the Biblical writers, 'God alone hath immortality.' But men are created by a God of infinite love and created for himself. They are, therefore, infinitely precious in his eyes. He cannot, being eternal Love, cease ever to hold them dear, nor consent to scrap them after three score years and ten. Their hope rests not in anything in themselves but in the unchangeable relationship of love in which they are created and held. As a writer on the Old Testament has expressed it, 'God's eternal life ensures the durability of man's communion with him.'[9]

At the risk of repeating much that is theological commonplace and yet which is still astonishingly unfamiliar, it will be useful to define more closely the Christian hope for the individual by further contrast with the previous doctrine. For it is still an almost universally cherished belief that the Immortality of the Soul is a tenet of the Christian faith, despite the fact that it rests on theological assumptions which are fundamentally at variance with the Biblical doctrines of God and man.

The Christian eschatology of the individual departs from the immortality doctrine discussed above at the following important points.

(*a*) Its hope of eternal life rests solely on its doctrine of God and not on its doctrine of man. There is nothing in man, however noble, which is not subject to death and

[9] H. Knight, *The Hebrew Prophetic Consciousness*, p. 173.

by nature corruptible: ' All flesh is as grass, *and all the glory thereof* as the flower of grass' (1 Pet. 1.24, quoting Is. 40.6). 'Ye shall not surely die'—the basis of the Plutonic hope—is the first lie recorded in Scripture (Gen. 3.4). Everything in man is finite and must return to dust—'but the word of the Lord endureth for ever' (1 Pet. 1.25; Is. 40.8). The essence of man and his personality according to the Biblical view rests in nothing in himself but in the fact that he is called to existence in a certain relationship with God. It is this ' word' spoken to him and to which his life is required to be the answer, that is eternal. It is a word of love which cannot cease nor let him go: it establishes a bond of responsibility which neither life nor death can sever. God will not, cannot, suffer his beloved one to see corruption, but, beyond the grave and gate of death, claims him for a life of eternal fellowship with himself.

(*b*) Since Christianity rests its doctrine of eternal life entirely on God and not on man, it has no place for any view of conditional immortality. The tendency of all doctrines which ground man's hope in his essential affinity with the things of the spirit is to limit it to those who are truly ' spiritual ' (*pneumatikoi*). The hope is for the initiated, for the philosopher, the yogi, for the man who has learnt how to die, for those who are not carnal, whose souls have not become quite overlaid with dross and clay. Immortality, indeed, is available to all, but how few there be that find it!

One can trace here the underlying suspicion that not all men *deserve* immortality. This is indeed the starting-point of the Christian doctrine. But it is applied far more radically. Christianity has no room for those who believe themselves immortal and despise others. It asserts outright that *no one* deserves eternal life. The desert of every man is *death*; all have sinned—there is no difference—and the wages of sin is death. The Gospel affirms, indeed, that man was not made to die, and that he knows it. 'To be called to spirit, to freedom, to fellowship, to unconditional responsibility—and yet to sink down to death: this contradiction man *ought* to feel. He *ought* to rebel against his dying as something unnatural.'[10] But whereas for the philosophical Idealist that is the ground of man's hope—' thou shalt not *surely* die '—for the Bible it is the ground of man's tragedy—he *must* die, in spite of everything.

In Adam *all* die; but in Christ *all* are made alive. That is the divine ' nevertheless,' beyond all hope or merit. It rests on no condition of virtue or spirituality, but solely on the unconditional love of God. Consequently, *all* will be raised; and this despite the perennial tendency of the religious to assert, both within Scripture and outside it, that there can be resurrection only for the righteous. But no amount of human sin, and no depth of unworthiness, can affect or deflect the loving purpose of God in Christ. And this means not only that all will be raised; it means, since God has elected all for *eternal* fellowship with himself, that he loves every man beyond any power of his to sin himself out of the relationship in which he is created. Against any view that some men, whether at death or at the last day, can render themselves incapable of an eternal destiny, the Christian faith asserts a love in God, unconditional and omnipotent, which makes the form of each man's personal existence for ever inalienable: the call of God is without repentance.

(*c*) All men will be raised; the relationship with God which makes humanity human is indestructible. But for that very reason all will be raised to a life-in-relationship, to a life from which no escape from God is possible. And for some that will be heaven, and for some that will be hell. Neither the doctrine of the immortality of the soul nor theories of survival (whether primitive or modern) have any place for an element of *judgment*.[11] For, ultimately, their conception is not of life with God, but of life with one's true self and other selves. Indeed, such doctrines can be, and have been, argued apart from any belief in God. But, for the Bible, eternal life is essentially and ineluctably to

[10] P. Althaus, *op. cit.*, p. 103.
[11] On this see further ' Preaching Judgment' in *On Being the Church in the World*, Chapter XII.

know God and to be with him. The exponent of immortality assumes too simply that immortality is in itself salvation. But that is to reckon without God and without sin. To be raised to live with God, without any possibility of surcease, may be the most unendurable torment.[12] But God wills nevertheless to have it so. For resurrection is his destiny for every man, whether he is worthy of it or not, whether he likes it or not. For it depends on God's *unconditional love*. But what strange kind of a love is this? Can a God of love be content that any should find that to live with him is hell, torment without remedy, without escape, and without end? If he cannot, what is the outcome? What finally is the end of the Lord towards the individual and the whole of the human race? Here we touch the ultimate issue of eschatology.

(d) But before this can be considered, there is a further great point of difference between the doctrine of immortality and that of resurrection which requires a more extended treatment. As, for the latter, the whole man dies, and not only the material part of him, so likewise the whole man will be raised and not merely the 'spiritual' in him. The Bible opposes the *immortality of the soul* with the *resurrection of the body*. An examination of this key doctrine will also serve to reveal the connection between the eschatology of the individual and the end of history as a whole, which is presupposed in the answer to the ultimate question just raised.

---

[12] This is what the Bible means by eternal death—not extinction, but, as Althaus puts it: 'Inescapable godlessness in inescapable relationship to God' (*op. cit.*, p. 183). 'If "eternal death" meant annihilation, God's judgment would be finite, limited by a saving "No more"' (p. 182).

CHAPTER IX

The Resurrection of the Body

The Resurrection of the Body is a doctrine which entered Christianity through the language of St. Paul. The first essential, therefore, is to understand what the Apostle meant when he used the word 'body' (*soma*).[1] It is one of the key words of his thought. Indeed, the whole of Pauline theology might well be written round it. It is from the body of sin and death that we are redeemed; it is through the body of Christ on the Cross that we are saved; it is into his body the Church that we are incorporated; it is by his body in the Eucharist that this fellowship is built up; it is in our bodies that the life of the Spirit has to be manifest; it is to a transforming of our body to the likeness of his glorious body that we are destined. The subtle links between the different uses of this word *soma* provide a clue to the profound unity of Pauline thought. For none of them can really be understood independently of the others.

Here, however, we must confine ourselves. It will be enough to begin by clarifying the meaning of *soma* in St. Paul's analysis of human personality.

Except in one instance (1 Thess. 5.23), St. Paul follows the twofold Hebraic division of man into soul and flesh, in preference to the threefold Greek division into body, soul, and spirit. For the Hebrew, 'spirit' is not a part of man's make-up as such. It is the Spirit of God which comes upon, enters, and dwells in the human personality, bestowing on man the possibility of a supernatural life of which as part of nature he is incapable. In later Old Testament thought, and supremely in the New Testament after Pentecost, this indwelling is seen no longer as the external, intermittent and highly selective invasion of special indi-

[1] For a much fuller treatment see my book, *The Body*.

viduals by the divine *ruach* (Spirit), but as an immanent and continuous moral presence. Consequently, one finds the word 'spirit' so closely identified with the true life of man which is the life of God in him that it can actually become qualified by personal pronouns, in phrases like 'my' spirit and 'yours.' Yet the natural man, Adam, is a living soul rather than a life-giving spirit (1 Cor. 15.45). Spirit (*pneuma*) is not a department of human psychology: it is a relationship of God towards man; though, in so far as a man responds to that relationship, he may with truth speak of 'his' spirit, the Spirit which has become his life.

The human person as such, apart from God's Spirit, can be regarded as soul (*psyche*) and as flesh (*sarx*). Though the two terms can each stand for the whole man, *psyche* corresponds more or less with the same term—the psyche—in modern science. It embraces that of man and his processes which come within the purview of the psychologist. *Sarx* corresponds to that of man and his processes with which the biologist is primarily concerned. The Hebrew was remarkably modern in refusing to make any hard and fast distinction between the two. He would have given ready assent to the idea of 'the physical basis of personality.' And, on the other hand, unlike some moderns, he would have insisted that in man there were no purely animal behaviour-patterns. The works of the 'flesh,' just because they were in human beings and not beasts, were never purely physical. The division between *sarx* and *psyche* was merely convenient. No theological (or scientific) distinction could be based on it. St. Paul uses *psychikos* and *sarkikos* indifferently to mean 'natural.' The real division came between these two on the one hand and *pneuma* on the other, which belonged to the realm of the supernatural and divine. Whereas for Platonism the *psyche* was on the godward side of the line, for St. Paul and the Hebrews generally it is quite definitely not. It is neither divine nor immortal, but as subject to corruption as the flesh.

The *soma* (or body), though again the word can be used interchangeably with *sarx*, is the whole psycho-physical unity of man as created for God. It is the nearest word in Greek for 'personality,' for which none of the ancients had a term. But it is personality, as it were, *ad extra*. It is not the inner essence of what, theologically, makes man a person. This, for the Hebrew, is always something outside man himself—the call of God to a relationship of unique responsibility to himself—and lies in the realm of Spirit. And, secondly, it is not personality as it has been defined abstractly in the Western philosophical tradition, especially since Descartes. It is not the 'self' prior to and apart from its relationships. *Soma* is the whole man constituted by the network of physical and mental relationships in which he is bound up with other persons and things.

There is here an important point of distinction between Hellenic and Hebraic anthropology. In Greek thought, the essence of man, that which makes him a man and not an animal, is his participation in a universal spirit or reason. That which gives him individuality is the body, the psycho-physical frame which contains and marks off, as it were, one unit of this universal rational nature and makes it that 'individual substance' which is one person and not another. 'A person is an individual substance of a rational nature,' said Boethius in his classic definition; to which the School-men added the rider, 'The principle of individuality is matter.' The body is what makes a man *a* man. In non-Christian Hellenic thought the body, and with it this division of the universal spirit into individual compartments, was regarded as evil or unreal or at any rate temporary. In Christian thought the resurrection of the body was asserted to insist that individuation is a good and divine thing—the frontiers between person and person reach up to heaven. The doctrine stood for the safeguarding of men's continued identity as complete and separate selves: there can, it declared, be no merging or absorption of personality in the communion of saints.

In the Hebraic doctrine of man the significance of body and spirit for individuality is reversed. The principle of individuation lies in man's existence as a spiritual being, in the relationship of each man to God which makes him what and who he is. A man is *a* man because God calls each person by his own name to an unrepeatable relatedness and an indivisible responsibility to himself, to return a unique answer to the Word of his Creator. The Spirit is not here an undifferentiated substance or universal nature, of which the individual partakes; it is a highly differentiating, individuating power of Love, dividing to every man severally as he wills.

The body, on the other hand, is, on this view, the symbol, not of individuality, but of solidarity. It is that which binds each individual, divinely unique as he is, in inescapable relatedness with the whole of nature and history and the cosmic order. It is the bond of continuity and unity between man and his environment, between individual and community, between generation and generation.

In passing, it may be noted that it is this Hebraic conception of the body that is the one supported by modern science. There is no complete individuality in nature, and no watertight compartments. To the biologist, the body is part of a continuous stream of plasm which passes unbroken from generation to generation. In this stream there are no fast frontiers between one personality and another, any more than a great river takes cognizance of the boundary between one state and the next. To the biochemist, the body is not a constant, isolable unit, but persists only in a continuous state of metabolic change and, in interaction with its environment, is completely transformed in the course roughly of each seven years.

To the psychologist, equally, the psyche is without hard frontiers and lacking the unity and identity which could make it legitimate to speak of it as an individual substance. Here, for instance, is the considered conclusion of Professor H. H. Price:[2] 'The phenomena of telepathy show that one mind is not separated from another by any sharp and clear-cut boundary. Imagine two minds which were in a state of

[2] 'Psychological Research and Human Personality,' *The Hibbert Journal*, January 1949, p. 109.

complete and continuous telepathic *rapport,* so that every experience of either directly affected the experiences of the other. Would there any longer be any sense in calling them two minds and not one? If the causal connection between two sets of mental states were as close as this, we should have to say that there was one mind in two bodies; just as, if there is a sufficient degree of *disconnection* between two groups of mental states, both of which are associated with the same body, we have to say that the mind animating that body has been split into two separate personalities. It comes to this: both *ad intra* and *ad extra* (if I may so put it) the unitariness of the human mind seems to be a matter of degree, and not a matter of all or none. In relation to other minds, it is without clear boundaries; and its internal coherence is greater or less in different circumstances, and never perhaps complete (some degree of dissociation occurs in all of us whenever we dream). In view of these facts, it is quite inappropriate, indeed, positively misleading, to say that the human mind is a substance.'

The frontiers of the *soma* (as of *sarx* and *psyche*) are blurred. That can readily be admitted in an understanding of man which does not find in it the principle of individuality. The ground of this latter is the particularizing Word of God calling into being a peculiar human relationship to himself. The apparatus of the body through which the individual's response to that Word must be given is not permanently or exclusively his own. Is is always, as it were, on loan to a man from the race and from nature: dust it is and to dust it shall return—not only once, but continuously. Sometimes that loan is not complete enough for the individual to give free or integrated response through the apparatus of this body. Here we are in the realm of abnormal and defective psychology, whose problems the Bible would regard as part of the larger and universal problem, namely, that this psycho-physical body is *never* the perfect instrument of the Spirit: it must be redeemed and transformed.

To return, now, to the Biblical usage of the word *soma.* ' The body ' does not stand for or stress the self-sufficiency,

self-determination or isolation of each man from his neighbour. It is used, rather, to symbolize the *corporate solidarity*
of every person in the natural, historical, and cosmic order,
whether this be unredeemed or redeemed.[3] In so far as
the body is simply natural and unredeemed, it represents
man's solidarity in sin and death. It is that which links all
men in the common sin and mortality of Adam, that which
binds man and nature in a shared futility and a common
suffering, that which, through the elemental forces of this
world, enslaves man to cosmic powers beyond his control.
It stands for the involvement of every human being in the
massa peccatrix, ' the body of sin ' (Rom. 7.24).[4]

The doctrine of the resurrection of the body is the
doctrine of the redemption and replacement of one solidarity
by another—the body of the old mortality by the body of
Christ. It is an assertion that no individual can be saved
apart from the whole. Through his body he is organically
linked with all other life and all other matter in the universe.
There is no redemption for the individual *out of* this mass,
but only in it and with it. The Christian gospel is not of
the rescuing of individuals out of nature and history (these
things themselves being considered simply as a vale of soul-
making), but the redeeming of all the myriad relationships of
creation into a new heaven and a new earth, the city of God,
the body of Christ (see Rom. 8.19-23; Phil. 3.21; etc.).

This interpretation of the Gospel, and its assertion by
the doctrine of the renewing of the body, is intimately associated with an element in the resurrection myth that is little
understood to-day and has been silently dropped from most

[3] E.g., Heb. 13.3 : ' Remember them that are in bonds as bound
with them; them that are evil entreated, as being yourselves also
in the body '; Rom. 7.4 : ' Ye also were made dead to the law
through the body of Christ; that ye should be joined to another,
even to him who was raised from the dead.' In each case the
implication of ' the body ' is solidarity.

[4] In this connection, it is significant how the singular (*soma*) is
used where we should expect the plural; e.g., in Rom. 8.23 :
' the redemption of our body '—not our bodies, but our body, the
old mortality, the whole lump of sin and death. Cf. Phil. 3.21 :
' the body of our humiliation.'

contemporary discussions. It is the insistence that the resurrection of the body must be placed at 'the last day' rather than immediately upon the individual's death.

Before, however, we can discuss the significance of this point, it is necessary to say something about two things that tend to confuse this issue for the modern man.

In the first place, it is as essential here, as in our previous discussion of the Second Coming, to make it quite clear that we are dealing with myth and not prediction. The doctrine of the resurrection of the body is misunderstood if it is regarded as a preview of what the future holds in store for the individual. Information about this no more forms part of the Christian revelation than prognostication about the end of history. Of course, *something* must actually happen to the individual, just as the world must end in one way and not in another. But it is not the function of Christian theology in either case to assert what this will be. The locus of its interest lies not in the future, but in the present. The doctrine of bodily resurrection is not forecast but myth. That is to say, it is the representation, in this as the most scientific form, of a truth which is integral to the total Biblical understanding of God's relationship to man, the truth, namely, that the *whole* of God's workmanship is of eternal value to himself and cannot ultimately be lost.

In exactly the same way, to speak of the 'postponement' of the resurrection of the body till the 'last day,' is to say nothing about the literal condition of the individual five minutes after death or at any other time. The gospel or redemption in Christ vouchsafes no answer to such inquiries: it is concerned to save and to challenge men in the present. But what it does do is to uncover a truth about God's dealing with men here and now and always which requires to be *represented* by such postponement in the myth. Where this representation drops out, it indicates, we shall argue, that this essential truth is being lost.

Such a statement will serve to differentiate our position from that of a literal fundamentalism, which has also stressed bodily resurrection only at the last day, but for a very different reason. It has seen the resurrection as literal prediction of a future body dependent upon the exhumation and redintegration of this present frame of flesh and bone. On this view it is obvious that the dead cannot have their body now, if only because they are ' there ' and it is ' here ' mouldering in the grave.

This position (which has been the traditional one both in Catholic and Protestant theology) finds itself involved in a host of unprofitable speculations concerning the precise relation between this body and the next, and about the state of the departed between death and resurrection. All such speculation is misplaced, and forms no part of the Christian doctrine of the Last Things, because it derives from a literalistic misunderstanding of the resurrection body. Theology is not in the least concerned with the transformation of the elements of one body into the other, as though the two were historically parallel; any more, for instance, than it is concerned with the metabolic relation between unfallen humanity of the Garden of Eden and the fallen man of history. The one does not pass into the other by biological sequence, as if each possessed the same factual status. Both the states of unfallen and of glorified humanity are related to man, the only man we know, not chronologically but interpretatively. In discussing the connection between them and the present body one is not dealing with a causal nexus : one is concerned with representing a relationship in myth which will be theologically sound, i.e. account as scientifically as possible for all the data in the Christian revelation of man.

If this is understood, one can go on to say that in the myth the relation between this present body and that of the resurrection must be represented both as one of non-identity and yet of continuity. On the one hand, the resurrection body cannot be pictured, as in spiritualism, simply as this present body going on (for it is certain that flesh and blood cannot inherit the kingdom of God); and yet it must be this body, this personality, transformed, and not another, if continuity of full personal existence is to be preserved (and not lost or interrupted, as, for instance, in theories of absorption or reincarnation).

And both these postulates of non-identity and continuity apply to the *whole* body. There is no room for speculation about which functions are 'taken up' and which not. Althaus, working with St. Paul's distinction between 'the belly' (*koilia*) and 'the body' (*soma*) in 1 Cor. 6.13 ff., makes this wise statement: 'The body is, on the one hand, wholly *koilia*, that is, the sum of the sensual functions, which make our earthly life possible; as such it passes away with this earthly world. On the other hand, the body is wholly *soma*, that is, the carrier and object of our action, expression, and form; as such it is a limb of the body of the risen Christ and will be raised with the personality. Because the one and the same body is *both koilia and soma*, concrete or objective expression of what dies, and what is preserved and purified through resurrection, is impossible.'[5]

[5] *Op. cit.*, p. 130. Such a principle of interpretation should be applied, for instance, to Mark 12.25: 'When they shall rise from the dead, they neither marry, nor are given in marriage, but are as angels in heaven.' This reply is intended to deny the validity for the resurrection life of the limitations and problems connected with the body as *koilia. In the flesh*, it is impossible for a woman to be *wife* to seven brethren at once. For such a relationship demands the whole consecration of time and attention upon one partner, and a second can only receive this at the expense of the first. It is, consequently, a relationship based on *exclusion*. It is only after the death of the first partner that a second union becomes possible that can be equally full without trespassing upon the fullness of the first. In a communion, however, no longer thus limited by space and time, it is possible to conceive a state where the completeness of marriage relationship with one partner does not rest only on a denial of the same complete relationship with another or others. The question, therefore, 'Whose wife shall she be?' then becomes irrelevant. It is a problem created by the limitation of the body as *koilia*.

What is wrong is when this text is extended to the body as *soma* and is made the basis for a doctrine that all distinctions of personal relationship based on marriage are obliterated in the kingdom of heaven. For such distinctions are part of the very form and substance of personality-in-relationship (*soma*). We cannot talk of history being 'taken up' into the kingdom of God if the

All this has taken us some way from our immediate intention, which is to clear up two sources of misapprehension in the way of understanding the doctrine of the Resurrection of the Body only at 'the last day.' The first source we have now dealt with, that of literalist fundamentalism. The second difficulty can be treated more briefly. It derives from the change of presupposition, interest, and emphasis which has necessarily occurred in thought about the resurrection of the body since the passing of the first-century situation.

St. Paul's discussion is dominated by the idea of the imminent return of Christ and the establishment of a Messianic reign upon earth, which for most of those he is addressing will occur *this side of the grave.* In the case of this majority, i.e., those still alive, he conceives no great difficulty : they will be already on the stage. But the dead in Christ cannot be cut off from the triumph of their Lord. For as Christians they are already risen men; for them death has been defeated; it cannot possibly stand in the way of their participation. But if the dead are to return, the question arises : 'With what body will they come?' (1 Cor. 15.35). For it is impossible to re-enter the terrestrial scene, however transformed it may be, without a body of some kind. St. Paul's answer is that *everybody* will undergo a change (whether they have fallen asleep or not) and that the body received will be not a ' natural' body but a ' spiritual ' body, adapted indeed to earthly conditions, but the perfect and transparent instrument of the Spirit.

But the modern problem has nothing to do with return to a quasi-terrestrial form of existence. Popular speculation is focused, rather, on the question ' with what body will they go?'—i.e., to ' heaven' (' Heaven ' is never in fact used in the

---

individualities of relationship that make it what it is are simply abolished. Much unnecessary distress has been caused by a false interpretation of this text to those who feel, rightly, that the particularity of relation between, say, husband and wife is something that cannot perish without destroying an element integral to the ' body ' of both.

Bible for the destination of the dying: it stands for the dwelling-place of God and of Christ and of those who even now share his eternal life). Consequently, discussion of the Resurrection of the Body has come to be pursued in terms of what happens at death. The reading of 1 Cor. 15 at funerals reinforces the impression that this chapter is about the moment of death: in fact it revolves around two points, 'the third day' and 'the last day.'

The matter can be otherwise expressed by saying that our mind, unlike St. Paul's, does not work naturally with a scheme of *two* resurrections—the resurrection *of Christians* to a (temporary) Messianic kingdom on earth, and the later, *general* resurrection of all men for the purpose of being judged worthy or unworthy of the ultimate kingdom of God. In his discussion of the resurrection of the body, St. Paul is referring solely to the *first* resurrection; whereas the modern age tries to apply his language, which is adapted to that, to a *single* resurrection thought of as following immediately upon death.

The idea of two kingdoms and two resurrections, though common to St. Paul and the Apocalypse, does not appear in the Gospels.[6] It is best viewed as an attempt to harmonize, under the form of successive events, the two elements of the myth emphasized by the prophets and apocalyptists respectively, namely, that the meaning of history must be vindicated *within* history and yet that the complete purpose of God must *transcend* history. The representation of this tension as two stages leads to error if taken literally. For us, the resurrection of the body (an essential element in the total eschatological myth) must be related to the *whole* doctrine of resurrection which does justice to both these emphases.

With these two preliminary observations required to set the discussion in correct perspective, we may now go on to the significance which the Biblical writers saw in the conception of bodily resurrection only as an *ultimate* event.

It will be useful to begin from a passage which on the

[6] See the discussion of the matter in Schweitzer's *The Mysticism of Paul the Apostle*, Chapter V.

face of it might appear to *deny* such a postponement. Indeed, it is to this passage that the modern view, if it refers to Scripture at all, makes its appeal. The relevant verses are 2 Cor. 5.1-8,[7] which in the Revised Version run:

> For we know that if the earthly house of our tabernacle be dissolved, we have a building from God, a house not made with hands, eternal, in the heavens. For verily in this we groan, longing to be clothed upon with our habitation which is from heaven: if so be that being clothed we shall not be found naked. For indeed we that are in this tabernacle do groan; being burdened; not for that we would be unclothed, but that we would be clothed upon, that what is mortal may be swallowed up of life. Now he that wrought us for this very thing is God, who gave unto us the earnest of the Spirit. Being therefore always of good courage, and knowing that, whilst we are at home in the body, we are absent from the Lord (for we walk by faith, not by sight); we are of good courage, I say, and are willing rather to be absent from the body, and to be at home with the Lord.

This is commonly interpreted to mean, in clear opposition to 1 Cor. 15, that our spiritual body is waiting for us to put on at the moment of death. H. L. Goudge, in his commentary on 2 Corinthians, disposes adequately of such an exegesis. He insists that to read this passage as primarily about the resurrection of the dead and the condition of the individual at the hour of death is to see it through modern spectacles. Here, as in 1 Cor. 15, St. Paul is primarily concerned with the situation of Christians at the Parousia, and this, and not the point of death, is the moment under discussion. At the Parousia, the great majority of Christians will, it is assumed, still be *alive*. St. Paul's language is governed by the presupposition that most of those to whom he is speaking will be 'clothed,' i.e., still in the body, and there-

[7] For a fuller exegesis of this passage, see *The Body*, pp. 75-8.

fore that 'clothed upon' is the right expression for the
resurrection; though he adds as an afterthought (and this
is surely, as Goudge insists, the true meaning of verse 3):
'if indeed it *is* as "clothed" and not as "naked" (i.e.,
already dead) that we shall be found (at the Parousia).'
St. Paul quite definitely asserts that the condition of the
dead until the day of the Lord *is* one of nakedness, of dis-
embodiment (verse 8), though that dismal state is more than
compensated for by their closeness to Christ. Bodily resurrection is something that does not and cannot occur till the
last day.

That, however, is not the entire truth (and here our
interpretation goes beyond Goudge). For the Church is
already living in the End. All Christians, *whether quick or
dead*, possess the earnest of the Spirit (verse 5; cf. Rom.
8.11, 23). Consequently, for the dead in Christ, their resurrection and their body are not *merely* future. It is true that
the redemption and transformation of the body is still, for
all of us, in its completeness a future state (Rom. 8.23;
Phil. 3.21). But it is also a fact that, proleptically, 'we *have*,'
whether we are alive or dead, 'a building from God, a house
not made with hands, eternal, in the heavens' (verse 1)—
namely, *the body of Christ*, the Church. This, and not their
usual interpretation as speaking of an individual resurrection
body, is, I believe, the primary meaning of these words.
Such language elsewhere in the New Testament, and it is
quite common,[8] is always used for the *Church*, the body of
Christ, the temple of the living God. Moreover, the unbroken connection between the closing verses of 2 Cor. 4
and the beginning of Chapter 5 makes it clear that the
Apostle is referring to something that is already an active
reality building up Christians here and now—not a body we
have only when we die, but the body of Christ, which is
not among the things that are decaying and will finally
be dissolved, but is eternal, and ours already in the Spirit,
renewing the inward man.

[8] For a useful collation of these passages, see Additional Note
H in E. G. Selwyn's commentary on *I Peter*.

The resurrection of the body, like the whole of the eschatological myth, describes, therefore, something that is both
a present possession and an ultimate hope. The one thing
it does not describe is something that is going to be acquired
upon the moment of death. That would be to give the hour
of death a decisiveness which for the New Testament it does
not possess.[9] The great ' moments ' upon which everything
turns, here as elsewhere, are the Resurrection and the Parousia.
    That the myth refuses to place the Resurrection of the
Body immediately after death is no accident. It is profoundly
important for the Hebraic understanding of eschatology. As
long as the Hellenic presuppositions about the significance
of the body for individuation are assumed, it cannot, indeed,
seem anything but foolishness. For to deny continuous
bodily existence would be to deny the persistence of self-
identity. But, on the Hebraic presuppositions, this does not
follow at all. Individuality does not depend on the body :
it rests in the individuating Word of God. The body
represents solidarity; and the denial of its redemption and
restoration immediately upon death stands for the great truth
that no one can fully be saved apart from his brother, or
indeed apart from the whole of creation.[10] It is only in the

    [9] On this see further ' Preaching Death ' in *On Being the Church
in the World,* Chapter XI.
    [10] In the Hellenic tradition of Christian theology this implication
of the Resurrection of the Body ceases to be stressed. The state
of blessedness for the individual comes when his period of purgatory is over and is independent of the restoration of the body,
which becomes a purely external addition : the essential man, as in
Platonism, is complete without it. (See the excellent discussion of
this in Althaus, *op. cit.,* pp. 138 ff.) Indeed, if it were not for
the belief that the resurrection body depends on the literal raising
of *this* body, which lies at the moment interred, there would seem
little in most medieval presentations of the doctrine to prevent
the teaching of an immediate restoration. The extent to which
' the body ' ceased to stand for the corporate solidarity of man
in nature and history is indicated by the later severance of the
doctrine of the resurrection of the body (which was retained) from
the doctrine of a renovated earth (which was rejected in favour of
a purely ' spiritual ' communion of saints). Cf. Althaus, *op. cit.,* p.
344.

last day when all things are restored that the new corporality will be complete.

Meanwhile, the process of redemption is the process of the building up of the body of Christ, 'unto a fullgrown man, unto the measure of the stature of the fulness of Christ . . . from whom all the body fitly framed and knit together through that which every joint supplieth, according to the working in due measure of each several part, maketh the increase of the body unto the building up of itself in love' (Eph. 4.13, 16). Each individual, when and as he comes into Christ, begins to put on the new man. The resurrection of the body begins, not at death, but at baptism (cf. 1 Cor. 15.29). What happens at death does not concern the new body, but the old. For it is then that this latter, representing the dissolving solidarity of the present order, is finally stripped away. Each person lies naked and responsible before God. The natural man at present sees all men 'according to the flesh,' in Adam, and in the comforting solidarity which that provides. God sees all men in Christ, and only in so far as they are in the solidarity of his body will they be 'at home' (2 Cor. 5.8). For ultimately there will be no other: the body of Christ is the only corporeity which is 'eternal in the heavens.' Not till a man has put on *that* will he know salvation; and not till *all* have found themselves in it, and everything is finally summed up in Christ, will this salvation be complete for any.

CHAPTER X

The End of the Lord

'Ye . . . have seen the end of the Lord, how that the Lord is full of pity and merciful' (Jas. 5.11). Such was the apostolic message. Christians *have seen* the end of the Lord. To them eschatology is neither the peering of curiosity nor the prising of argument into a future state. The *telos* has been declared in the *fait accompli* of Jesus Christ. In him ' it is finished,' into him all things have been gathered up. Whenever the *finis* may come, there can be no other end to the universe : God will be all in all. The New Testament asserts the final *apokatastasis*, the restoration of all things, not as a daring speculation, nor as a possibility, but as a reality —a reality that shall be and must be, because it already is. It already *is*, because it is grounded in what has been, the decisive act of God, once and for all, embracing every creature. ' In Christ *shall all* be made alive' (1 Cor. 15.22), because ' through one act of righteousness the free gift *came* unto *all men* to justification of life' (Rom. 5.18). St. Paul makes it clear that his vision of the end is simply the complete realization of something that, essentially, has already been realized at the Resurrection. In Eph. 1.20-2 he speaks of the power of God in raising Christ from the dead, when he ' made him to sit at his right hand in the heavenly places, far above all rule, and authority, and power, and dominion, and every name that is named, not only in this world, but also in that which is to come : and he put all things in subjection under his feet, and gave him to be head over all things to the Church.' His myth of the end is only the translation of this accomplished fact into the future. The promise of universal restoration is assured by the past : there cannot be any other outcome. ' Then cometh the end, when he [Christ] shall deliver up the kingdom to God, even the Father; when he shall have abolished all rule and all authority and power. For he must reign, till he hath put all his enemies under his feet. The last enemy that shall be abolished is death. For, he put all things in subjection under his feet. But when he saith, All things are put in subjection, it is evident that he is excepted who did subject all things unto him. And when all things have been subjected unto him, then shall the Son also himself be subjected to him that did subject all things unto him, that God may be all in all' (1 Cor. 15.24-8).

But equally, in the New Testament, there is another myth of the End, which seems to point to a very different issue: 'When the Son of man shall come in his glory, and all the angels with him, then shall he sit on the throne of his glory and before him shall be gathered all the nations: and he shall separate them one from another, as the shepherd separateth the sheep from the goats: and he shall set the sheep on his right hand, but the goats on the left. . . . And these shall go away into eternal punishment: but the righteous into eternal life' (Matt. 25.31-3, 46).

On the one hand, universal restoration; on the other, a clear division between the saved and the lost. How are we to hold these two myths together? For that is what we must do; since it is clear that *both* of them rest on *realities* of the present situation. 'God sent not the Son into the world to judge the world; but that the *world* should be saved through him' (John 3.17)—there is the guarantee of universal cosmic redemption. And yet, in the next verse: 'he that believeth on him is not judged: he that believeth not hath been judged already' (John 3.18)—there is the inevitable dualism.

If the two myths are taken as literal forecasts of what is to happen at the end of the world, then clearly they are incompatible: either one or the other must be the actual issue. But that is to misunderstand their character as myth. They are not forecasts, but represent alike elements in the total Christian understanding of the End which must be retained together. Both are there, and it must be accepted as axiomatic that no solution can be entertained which is

based on an exclusion of half the data. Too often each
side of the case has been argued with complete conviction
only because it fails to do justice to the evidence against it.

But if this condition is firmly adhered to, what are the
possibilities? How can these two New Testament assertions
be reconciled? It has in fact been attempted in four ways.

The first solution need not detain us long. It is the
Calvinistic view that the two truths represent two different
divine decrees for two separate sets of persons. All will
be saved whom God has created for salvation; but others,
equally, will be damned whom he has destined to that end.
This view must be rejected as unbiblical. It rests on a misunderstanding of Rom. 9.22-3: 'What if God, willing to
show his wrath, and to make his power known, endured with
much long-suffering vessels of wrath fitted unto destruction:
and that he might make known the riches of his glory upon
vessels of mercy, which he afore prepared until glory.' St.
Paul here never says that there are two equal divine decrees.
Whereas he asserts certainly that God has prepared vessels
of mercy unto glory, the alternative is pure supposition
('What if God . . .?'). Moreover, the suggestion is *not* that
he had prepared vessels unto destruction (an impossible
thought even as a hypothesis), but that he 'endured with
much long-suffering vessels of wrath fitted unto destruction'
(i.e., vessels that had made themselves worthy only of destruction)—a very different idea.[1]

The second solution is to hold that the two myths stand
for the two issues which eternally remain open. They are
to be held together, not as realities, but as possibilities.
It is not denied that universal restoration *may* be the end:
it is possible that all men will be won. But no dogmatism
is here in place. For equally it is possible that salvation
may finally be declined. Who are we to say in advance?
We must preserve both the freedom of God and the freedom
of man.[2]

---

[1] A good discussion of this is to be found in Brunner, *The Christian
Doctrine of God*, pp. 323-34.
[2] This is the view of Althaus, Brunner, and also of Professor

But of all positions, though it sounds the most humble, it is in fact that most subtly unbiblical. For the New Testament never says that God *may* be all in all, that Christ *may* draw all men unto himself, but that he *will*. And to assert that he will is not human dogmatism, but to hold fast to the fundamental declaration of the Gospel of the effective election of all men in Christ. Equally, the Bible never says that some men *may* depart into eternal punishment, but that they *shall*. To interpret these myths as *possibilities* rather than realities is to base one's eschatology not on divine *fact*, which has foreclosed all possibilities, but on human speculation which ignores the decisiveness of what Christ *has done*.

The third solution has the merit of holding both the elements together as realities and yet of retaining the unity of the divine decree. But it achieves its synthesis at too easy a level, and only at the cost of a genuinely Christian doctrine of God.

This is the traditional position represented by those councils and theologians of the Church who have condemned the doctrine of universal salvation as heretical. Their answer has been to say that God *will* be all in all *despite* the damnation or destruction of many of his creatures.

Now between this view and any form of universalism there must be war to the death. For the universalist asserts: 'The God I believe in, the God I see in Christ, *could not* be all in all *in these conditions*: such victory *could not* be the victory of a God of love.' We are here in the presence of two doctrines of God, and between them there can be no peace. It is one of the virtues of Brunner's treatment of this subject in his *Christian Doctrine of God*[3] that he states this final incompatibility so clearly. The truth of universalism is not the peripheral topic of speculation for which it has often been taken. If God is what ultimately he asserts himself

T. F. Torrance in his article (replying to one of mine) in *The Scottish Journal of Theology*, September, 1949.
[3] Pp. 334-6.

to be, then *how* he vindicates himself as God and the *nature* of his final lordship is at the same time the answer to *what* he essentially is. The truth or falsity of the universalistic assertion, that in the end he is Lord entirely of a world *wanting* his lordship, is consequently decisive for the whole Christian doctrine of God. If it is false, as Brunner believes, then he is right in scenting and exposing it as a ' menacing heresy, endangering the Biblical faith.'

The traditional position is defended by St. Thomas Aquinas in his *Summa Theologiae* (Ia. XIX, 6). He supports the thesis ' God's will is always fulfilled,' despite the Scriptural assertion that God ' willeth that all men should be saved and come to the knowledge of the truth,' of which he says simply ' *hoc non ita evenit,*' it does not turn out like that. He offers three interpretations of the text which might bring it into line with what he regards as observed fact. The first two are merely sophistical, and he rests nothing on them. The third, which he cites from John of Damascus, runs as follows. A distinction must be drawn between the antecedent or absolute will of God and his consequent or conditioned will (without implying by this any idea of temporal antecedence or change of mind). Absolutely, God wills all to be saved, in the same way as a just judge desires in general that each man should live rather than die. But in the same way as the judge must will that a homicide should be hanged, so God's consequent will is that some should be damned, since his justice demands it (*secundum exigentiam suae justitiae*). What, therefore, God does in general will to happen may not take place, since there are circumstances in which to will it would mean that he would be willing something evil or unjust. But what God does actually (i.e., consequently) will in any given situation always comes to pass. In this way St. Thomas seeks to combine the possibility of damnation with the complete fulfilment of the divine will. The exercise of freedom to reject salvation does not destroy the omnipotence of God.

The essential contention of this argument, which in some form or other must be that of all who would wish to defend the same position, is that what is apparently a change of will (from saving to damning) is based, not in any external inhibition of the divine power, but in the internal constancy of God's nature itself. There is no contradiction of this nature in the condemning of those he created for love: rather, this is the expression of its very consistency. The contradiction would be that God should save those who by their sin have made themselves worthy only of punishment. For then he would be false to his own nature of *holy* love.

Let us analyse this contention a little more closely. The assumption that underlies it is that in his love God wills all men to be saved, but that his justice requires many to be damned. Many would wish to cover up such a bald antithesis, but it is, nevertheless, ineluctably present in some form. St. Thomas, indeed, would have no objection to the statement as it stands. But it could be altered to present a more acceptable appearance, in which case it would run something like this. The divine power is not defeated by the fact that God's antecedent will of love is not fulfilled. For it is a power which is equally one of justice. A failure to convert is not really or finally a failure: the divine nature is still vindicated in condemnation. God's glory and power are always perfected, whether in the life or death of the creature, whether in mercy or in judgment. In each case he is omnipotent; he has not failed.

But under whatever form or disguise it appears, this solution cannot satisfy, because it cannot preserve the absolute identity of the divine love and the divine justice. For, ultimately, these are not two parallel attributes, each of which stands for a different requirement of God's nature. Rather is his justice a quality of his love, a characterization of its working. His is a love of cauterizing holiness and of a righteousness whose only response to evil is the purity of a perfect hate. Wrath and justice are but ways in which such love must show itself to be love in the face of its denial. If it appeared in any other form, it would be less than perfect love. It is most important to hold to the fact that justice is in no sense a substitute for love, which comes into operation

when the other has failed to be effective. The impression
is often given that God has reserves of power upon which
he could fall back if the power of love were to fail, that
souls that cannot be won to a free response fall under a
judgment condemning them to involuntary destruction.[4] But
God has no power but the power of love, since he has
no purpose but the purpose of love and no nature but the
nature of love. If that fails, he fails. Justice is no second
line of defence: it has no power of its own. For it is
nothing other than love being itself, love in the face of
evil, continuing to exercise its own peculiar power.

Unless this is understood, not only does love become
sentimental and forgiveness immoral, but justice becomes
sub-Christian. A view of the divine justice is introduced
which can be satisfied with a purely negative assertion of
its rights in the condemnation of a sinner. It is regarded
as *in no sense a failure* on God's part if some men are
committed to eternal punishment or death, because therein
the divine justice is fully vindicated.[5] But no Christian
could acquiesce in such a *purely* retributive theory or regard
the sending of a criminal to the gallows as reflecting no
failure except in the man himself. It would be impossible
for a Christian judge to derive entire satisfaction from such
a 'vindication' of justice or to say that he wills the man's
death *simpliciter* (St. Thomas's word), without, that is, any
qualms or reservation or sense of frustration. So neither could
any Christian ascribe such an attitude to God. Just as every
verdict of condemnation in the courts is at the same time

[4] Cf. Brunner, *The Mediator*, p. 551: 'He wishes to make
himself known as love, as far as this is possible; but he must
also make himself known as the holy righteous Judge when
this is inevitable.'

[5] 'It is like saying that a state which was obliged to keep
half its citizens perpetually in prison would be as ideal a father-
land as one in which complete absence of crime kept the prisons
perpetually empty—provided only that the penal laws were ad-
ministered with equal justice in the two cases' (J. Baillie, *op. cit.*,
p. 244).

a confession of failure on the part of the society which
pronounces it, so every final damnation on the part of
God would speak the frustration of the omnipotence of his
love. Precisely because God's justice is always the sternness
of his *love*, such an outcome can never be its vindication,
nor indeed anything but its hopeless defeat. For death or a
purely retributive punishment (which eternal punishment
must by definition be) is the completest contradiction and
denial of love. Because his justice is in no sense antithetical
to his love, or even independent of it, but a very way of
its working, it is impossible that it should ever be content
with a purely negative assertion of itself. Judgment can never
be God's last word, because if it were, it would be the word
that would speak his failure. Judgment is, indeed, absolutely
necessary, as that through which alone sinful man can hear
the word of mercy. But the sole possible function of judgment
can be to enable men to receive the mercy which renders it
superfluous. God is the eternal 'Yea,' and if his last
word is any other than his first—a creative, affirming 'Let
there be!'—then his love is defeated and he is not omnipotent.
But that word of affirmation can only be pronounced upon
a creation which is in every respect 'very good.' Only if
and when all men respond with that 'Yes' which they are
called into being to give, can God utter the final '*consum-
matum.*'

In the last resort there is no way of avoiding the conclusion that any modification of the antecedent will of God
to save all implies a concession to a power outside himself.
One may work in terms of the demands of justice and love
and thus persuade oneself that the modification is compelled
by an internal rather than an external necessity. But the
idea of a consequent will cannot succeed in clearing itself
of the suspicion of being in some degree a falling away
from the antecedent, simply because the justice which it
embodies is but one element abstracted and isolated from
God's holy love. The will to forgive is quenched, and
God satisfies himself with stopping at the point of condemnation. And what is the reason? None other than that his

power to forgive is limited by the recalcitrance of the sinner. There could be nothing in God himself which would induce him to be content with this second best. The assertion that the divine power is completely vindicated as omnipotent in negative judgment is simply an attempt to cover up and justify what is really a disastrous failure. For, antecedently, God's will extends beyond judgment to life. His power is his omnicompetence to fulfil his purpose of love. And if it should not work out, the modifying factor must be sought, not within God's nature, but outside it. Nothing *in God* would make him will anything but life for all in any circumstances. The slightest modification would be a monument to the power of self-will to resist the divine love even to the uttermost. This power would have shown itself to be stronger than God and thereby have reared a final disproof of the omnipotence of his love. Whether he had to condemn to extinction one or millions, God would have failed and failed infinitely. For love could not will such a thing, nor contemplate the prospect of it with anything but abhorrence. Whether this failure is represented simply as the bounding of his omnipotence of love, or as a resort to a power of compulsion other than that of love, it makes no difference. In either case a contradiction would be set up within the divine being: God would simply cease to be God.

The final verdict, then, on this solution is that it merely *conceals* the split within the nature of God which Calvin externalized in the double decree, and that it conceals it only at the expense of the divine omnipotence. It cannot succeed in showing that if all are not saved God is still all in all *as love*. It is unsatisfactory, and unscientific, as an eschatology because it fails to vindicate in its view of the end the complete character of God revealed in Jesus Christ. The end of the Lord here is not '*full* of pity and merciful.'

CHAPTER XI

All in All

The remaining answer to the question concerning the ultimate issue of things is that of Universalism—the answer that God will be all in all because the whole world will be restored sinless to that relationship with him in which and for which he made it.

The universalist position has often been defended in ways and in forms which do it little credit. It has been grounded in the doctrine of man, in the requirements of human reason or the demands of human longing. But the sole basis for such a doctrine, as more than wishful thinking, is the work of God in Christ. It is this and this alone which transfers it from the realm of daring speculation or moral postulate into the field of faithful assurance.[1] There is no ground whatever in the Bible for supposing that all men, simply because they are men, are 'going the same way'—except to hell. Once again, it is solely the divine 'nevertheless,' inter-

---

[1] The contrast of outlook between the man who is 'in Christ' and the man who is not is vividly portrayed by comparing two contemporary documents from the first century A.D., II Esdras and the Epistle to the Romans. The former contains a most moving dialogue on the universalist issue which is too long to summarize here (Chapters 8 and 9). Its author is clearly a man whose whole theodicy desperately demands the ultimate salvation of all men. Yet the traditional view-point, represented by the voice of God, is too strong for him. He remains morally unconvinced by it, nevertheless can find no solid ground on which to base his own hope. The matter is finally dropped in a most inconclusive state, and appeal is made to the ultimate mystery into which all things must run out. How different is the tone of the same appeal to the mystery of God with which St. Paul ends his assertion of the universal scope of the redemption in Christ: 'O the depth of the riches both of the wisdom and the knowledge of God! how unsearchable are his judgments, and his ways past tracing out. . . . For of him, and through him, and unto him, are all things' (Rom. 11.33, 36).

vening beyond any expectation and merit, on which the Christian hope rests. If universalism is asserted on *this* ground, it can certainly lay claim to Biblical support. But it can finally establish itself only if it also preserves intact two other truths upon which the Bible is equally insistent. These are the reality of human freedom and the seriousness of hell. Let us therefore press these two conditions to the full; for without them no universalist eschatology can hope to convince.

First, then, the condition of freedom. Must not the necessary salvation of all involve an ultimate denial of human liberty? Can anything be expected from an attempt to make sense of a love which works by necessity? If all *must* be saved, can any be *saved*, in the only sense that makes the operation a work of love? If freedom and the ultimate capacity for refusal are infringed, what profit is there in such a work of salvation for a God of love? We should remember Kierkegaard's warning: ' It would help very little if one persuaded millions of men to accept the truth, if precisely by the method of their acceptance they were transferred into error.'[2]

This warning must be taken with all possible seriousness. Any solution which in any way compromises the fact of freedom stands self-condemned. For without freedom love cannot be love. Love to be a force at all demands the exercise of freedom. One cannot move a chair by loving it, but only a person who is perfectly free not to be moved if he does not wish to be. Love is peculiarly love and its power purely that of love only when this capacity to flout it is presupposed in all its integrity. Depreciate this in the least degree, and love is impotent. Nothing is so helpless as love which can enlist no co-operation. If it cannot draw out men's wills to free response, then it has no other resource : it is finished.

This unswerving insistence on the inviolability of freedom must be maintained from beginning to end if all that follows is not to fall away into self-contradiction and futility.

[2] *Concluding Unscientific Postscript,* p. 221.

And this insistence is not merely in the interests of human liberty: it is equally necessary in order to safeguard any Christian doctrine of God. For it is evident that God, if we may say so, has as much interest in the preservation of our freedom as ever we have ourselves, even in our most self-assertive moods. For if his omnipotence is to be *acknowledged* (and that is the only way in which an omnipotence of love could become effective and victorious), then the freedom required for the acknowledgment must be preserved right to the very end. The very act of submission is an act of freedom and embodies the assertion of its eternal integrity.

This rock of liberty, then, must stand. Are there any indications that an all-compelling love could possibly leave it intact? Perhaps an analogy from human relationships may help at this point—not to substantiate the *truth* of universalism (which rests entirely on the God who is revealed in Christ), but to make its truth less baffling for our imaginations to grasp.

It is probable that the mental picture usually conjured up of the relation between divine omnipotence and human freedom is that of two irresistible forces each pulling in opposite directions. If, *per impossibile*, one were to gain a painful inch here or there, it could only be at the expense of the other's loss: submission to the power of God must involve the abandonment of the freedom of man. But have we any reason to think that this is at all an accurate picture of what happens when will meets will in the personal relationship of love? Surely, it is grossly misleading.

We all know times, when a man or woman really shows his or her love for us, whether it be in some costly manifestation of forgiveness or self-sacrifice or in some small act of kindness or consideration, that we feel constrained to respond —we cannot help ourselves, everything within us tells us that we must. Our defences are down, the power of love captures the very citadel of our will, and we answer with the spontaneous surrender of our whole being. Yet, at the same time, we know perfectly well that at such moments we can, if we choose, remain unmoved; there is no physical compulsion to commit ourselves. Everyone may point to instances in which he has been constrained to thankful response by the overmastering power of love. And yet, under this strange compulsion, has anyone ever felt his freedom infringed or his personality violated? Is it not precisely at these moments that he becomes conscious, perhaps only for a fleeting space, of being himself in a way he never knew before, of attaining a fullness and integration of life which is inextricably bound up with the decision drawn from him by the other's love? Moreover, this is true however strong be the constraint laid upon him; or, rather, it is truer the stronger it is. Under the constraint of the love of God in Christ this sense of self-fulfilment is at its maximum. The testimony of generations is that here, as nowhere else, service is perfect freedom.[3]

When faced by an overpowering act of love, we realize how absurd it is to say that the freedom and integrity of our moral personality are safeguarded only if we set our teeth and determine not to allow ourselves to be won to its service. If, then, we do not lose, but rather find, our freedom in yielding to the constraining power of love, is there anything to be gained for the cause of liberty by demanding that when it is under the control of self-will it shall in the end be stronger than when it is under the control of love? May we not imagine a love so strong that ultimately no one will be able to restrain himself from free and grateful surrender? If the miracle of the forcing of pride's intransigence, which is no forcing but a gentle leading, can be achieved in one case (St. Paul would say, in my case), who are we to say that God cannot repeat it in all? One by one, may not each come to the point at which he finds himself constrained to confess in the words of Charles Wesley:

[3] 'Freedom' is, of course, here being used in a deeper sense than 'freedom to choose.' But the point is that it presupposes the elementary freedom rather than supersedes it. On this cf. K. E. Kirk's discussion of Augustine's profound analysis of grace as *love* in *The Vision of God*, pp. 343-5.

I yield, I yield,
I can hold out no more;
I sink by dying love compelled
To own thee conqueror!

But, it will be said, in all this there is still presupposed the real possibility that the power of self-will *could* be the stronger, even though we may admit that a universal victory of love would not in any degree imperil freedom. At the end of the process it would not be the fact that all have been saved, but the fact that all had to be saved, which would throw doubt on the validity of what had been achieved. The knowledge that, since God is what he is, the result could not have been different, seems to cut at the very root of freedom. A very powerful love which in the end carried the day by winning all to itself—yes. But an omnipotent love which knew from the beginning that it could not but conquer—where does that leave room for the reality of decision?

Let us go back again to our human loves, and call to mind how it has been with each one of us. We have known what it is to be confronted by a love too strong to resist. We had no intention of yielding one whit of our proud independence. And yet we fell: it was too great for us. It forced us to a free acknowledgment of its power. And how wonderful that moment of surrender was! We felt that that was the moment for which we had been waiting in order to become ourselves; we knew then that we had been born for just such an act as this. And yet, as the weeks passed, there still seemed so much of us that was not bound over and committed, so much that we would far rather surrender to the other's keeping but with which we could not bring ourselves to part. At intervals we felt that love overmastering us here a little, there a little more. But the process appeared so slow—and so uncertain. What ground was there for supposing that the complete surrender for which we yearned would ever be made possible to us? Suppose that other love, though so much greater than anything we could command, was simply not powerful enough ever finally to win the last fastness of our selfish resistance? Could we ever be sure that we should attain that which we knew to be the purpose of our life, but which we realized equally we could never reach except we were drawn from without? What if that other power might not prove quite equal to it? Should we be faced with the prospect of life's meaning frustrated at the last great encounter? Thus we reflected. And we knew that others too, could we but penetrate their deepest anxieties, must also be standing before this possibility, looking into it and wondering.

And then we seemed to hear a voice, which told us we need have no fear. It spoke of another love, which, though we knew it not, had all the while been meeting us in that love we knew. It was this love that had really been drawing us to itself and imparting to us the sense of returning to our long home. For it was that from which we had come, and in which, all unknowing, we had been living, and which now at length had begun to reclaim us for its own. And when we heard this, we took courage and put away our fears. For then we knew. We knew this love, that it was none other than the infinite love of God. And we laughed that we had ever allowed ourselves to think that there might not be a power without us great enough to conquer those last shreds of our pride and independence. For we knew that the power of *this* love could experience no bounds at all. Sooner or later, as we let it, it would bring us back to the haven where we would be. We rejoiced to know that we could not stop it, though we could not always trust ourselves not to wish to stop it. But in the end we knew that even this desire that it should not conquer would be taken from our willing hearts.

And with this assurance we were brought to the knowledge that with those others also, of whom we had thought before, it was the same. For even though they might be men who, like ourselves, thought not to know anything of the love of God, and who might meet but little love in those around them, yet we were persuaded that all of them would at last come to desire that same love as that by which we had been found. For we saw in that love, crucified for every man, a power which could not but draw all to itself, so gracious was it and insupportable for sinful men to behold. And with this vision of the sureness of God's victory, when all would freely own his sway, we returned to the world content. The knowledge that it must needs take place did nothing to disturb the certainty of our freedom. For we knew that this surrender was in no way contrary to it, but rather that in it alone could we discover our true liberty. And our assurance of it did but establish our hope, and the hope of all men, beyond the power of anything whereby we sinners might be able to prevent it.

It is in some such vision as this that most of us perhaps have come, if we have come at all, to the knowledge of the strange compulsion of God's love and to the assurance that its necessary victory would not abrogate, but simply release, our freedom. It has deliberately been put in terms of personal experience and not of argued statement. For it is only from the point of view of the subject in actual personal relation with God and other people that these things make sense. This is simply another way of saying with Kierkegaard that ' truth is subjectivity,' or with Buber that reality is found only in the *I-Thou* relationship of meeting. Directly one begins to consider the matter objectively, with the eye of the scientist or the spectator, the truth eludes one. Brunner himself has shown in his brilliant little book, *Truth as Encounter*, what shipwreck has been made in theology by trying to express in ' objective ' terms what is revealed and known only to the subject-in-meeting. Freedom is essentially something that belongs to, and is only real in, the world of the *Thou*. Attempt to net it within the categories of logic and scientific thought, and it slips through the mesh. It eludes the schema of cause and effect and cannot be contained within the simple disjunction of the law of non-contradiction. Objective reason always demands : either grace or free-will (or first one and then the other), either the divine omnipotence or the liberty of man. But a theology which is true to the personal realities it attempts to systematize must refuse this disjunction. It is bound to bear around with it the open wound of the paradox, that resolute assertion of ' both-and ' within the very body of the logic of non-contradiction. It must never close this wound. For the paradox is the reminder that, to be true, it must always remain open to that world of freedom and decision and personal encounter whose realities can never be contained within the co-ordinates of scientific thinking. In this *Thou*-world the assertion of ' both-and ' sets up no tensions. However much it may puzzle and irritate the philosopher, to the subject in gracious relation to God there is no felt contradiction between what he does and what God does in him. The difficulties which arise when this activity is schematized in terms of cause and effect, of the action and reaction of forces which are equal and opposite, simply do not exist for him. Similarly, to the Christian in the personal relationship of faith to God, the knowledge that the divine victory of love is necessary brings, not conflict and debate, but joy and peace in believing. For he sees this necessity as in no way inimical to freedom, but rather its very substantiation and assurance.

This difference of standpoints explains a puzzling character-istic that clings to all doctrines of predestination, whether of a single or double divine decree. It is a common observation about both Calvinists and universalists that their actions do not appear to follow logically from their theories. If one is bound to go to heaven (or hell) in the end, why trouble further about anything? That would seem the natural conclusion. Yet neither of these classes of men appears to be characterized by any less moral earnestness. They reveal a concern for converting and improving the world at least as serious as that of other Christians. This is usually re-garded merely as a notable and inexplicable fact, though often with the insinuation that they cannot really believe what they profess.

But the divergence is not in truth so very strange. It simply marks the difference between the ' subjective ' and 'objective' standpoints. From the point of view of objective logic, the exercise of the divine omnipotence renders superfluous, even if it does not eliminate, any effective human action or co-operation. Looked at 'objectively,' therefore, the consistent line of conduct would simply be to enjoy life and let things take their course. But to the subject in the *Thou*-relation of decision, the matter looks very different. The reality and significance of human responsibility is heightened rather than diminished. The knowledge that one is the object of another human being's love, who, whatever one may do, will continue to love and to cherish, is not the signal to seize the opportunity for careless and thoughtless living. Rather, the knowledge brings with it an overwhelming constraint to pursue precisely the opposite course.[4] It is only the man who does not really love, who looks at the matter 'objectively,' to whom the 'logical' course of action could possibly suggest or commend itself. So it is in our dealing with God. It is only those who do not know grace, in the sole way in which it can be known, i.e., 'subjectively,' to whom the exhortation to 'sin that grace may abound' can have the least plausibility. There is no real need to treat seriously the objection to universalism that it is morally or spiritually debilitating. The objection rests upon a misunderstanding into which no one who makes an existential profession of the belief is in any danger of falling.[5]

[4] Cf. Wisdom 15.2: 'For even if we sin, we are thine, knowing thy dominion; but we shall not sin, knowing that we have been accounted thine.'
[5] The Thirty-nine Articles of the Church of England clearly recognize the different effect of any doctrine of predestination upon those who are 'in' the truth and those who are not: 'As the godly consideration of Predestination, and our Election in Christ, is full of sweet, pleasant, and unspeakable comfort to godly persons, and such as feel in themselves the working of the Spirit of Christ, mortifying the works of the flesh, and their earthly members, and drawing up their mind to high and heavenly things, as well because it doth greatly establish and confirm their faith of eternal Salvation to be enjoyed through Christ, as because it doth fervently kindle their love towards God: So, for curious and carnal persons, lacking the Spirit of Christ, to have continually

From this point it is possible to go on to consider the second condition which any sound doctrine of universalism must satisfy. Can it do justice to that other element in the myth which requires insistence on the reality of hell? There is a dimension of seriousness which Christianity introduces into the question of existing which, as Kant once stressed, is bound up with its uncompromising dualism, not merely between heaven and earth, but between heaven and hell. These are the two poles between which every choice has to be made; and as a critic of universalism has put it: 'It is the infinite urgency of the situation that life and death hang in the balances and that it is possible to choose death as well as life. No doctrine that cuts the nerve of that urgency in the Gospel can be a doctrine of love, but only an abiding menace to the Gospel and to mankind.'[6] To those words anyone who would be faithful to the New Testament must subscribe.

But is this an urgency which the doctrine of universal salvation must deny? It is not, if the existential viewpoint is maintained from which alone the belief can be held. Directly the doctrine becomes a matter of interesting, objective speculation, then to say that all men will be won is to cut the vital nerve. This is why Jesus refused an objective answer to such a question: 'And one said unto him, Lord, are they few that be saved? And he said unto them, Strive to enter in by the narrow door: for many, I say unto you, shall seek to enter in, and shall not be able' (Luke 13.23-4). He insists on recalling each man to take his stand as 'subject' before the choice that confronts him. For it is not till then that *any* can be saved, let alone all. And to the man in this position the door is narrow. Any suggestion that it is wide and that there is plenty of time,

---

before their eyes the sentence of God's Predestination, is a most dangerous downfall, whereby the Devil doth thrust them either into desperation, or into wretchedness of most unclean living, no less perilous than desperation' (Art. XVII).

[6] T. F. Torrance, *op. cit.*

still less that all are bound to find their way through it, is a suggestion of the Devil.

To the man in decision—and that means to all men, always, right up to the last hour—hell is in every way as real a destination as heaven. Only the man who has genuinely been confronted by both alternatives can be saved. To preach heaven alone, as it is asserted the universalist must, is to deny men the possibility of salvation. For salvation is a state of having chosen; and, in the moment of choice (and no man can ever say: 'I am safe, I *have* chosen'), both alternatives are existentially as real. Eternal life is only for those who have passed through the valley of decision, 'between the last blue rocks,'[7] where acceptance and rejection are equally terrible possibilities. As long as a man presumes that the truth of universalism relieves him of reckoning with hell or making a decision, then he is not even on the road to the valley—or, rather, he has implicitly chosen hell. If, therefore, the universalist insists on the seriousness of choice, and consequently on the reality of an alternative, it is because he sees in desperate earnestness the nature of truth as subjectivity: it is not because he regards hell as an indispensable piece of bluff required to keep men moral.

But it is not enough to say that hell is a genuine *possibility*, and then go on to assert that the other alternative alone is a *reality*. For that is not to treat the two myths with equal seriousness. The one thing, indeed, we cannot say about hell is that it is a possibility. According to the one myth, it is an impossibility; according to the other, it is a reality. The solution of this paradox is not to be found in a compromise which in fact succeeds only in denying both statements. The two positions must be held together, not resolved into a third. How can this be?

It can only be if it is clearly seen that the two myths represent two different standpoints. They are not to be understood as parallel 'objective' statements of the final outcome of the universe. In this case, of course, one must be true and the other false. To take them as such alternative predic-

[7] T. S. Eliot, 'Ash Wednesday', *Collected Poems, 1909-62.*

tions and then to try and hold them together is necessarily to invite the theological errors discussed in the last chapter. The two myths represent, rather, the two sides of the truth which is in Jesus. The one says: 'Christ is all in all, and always will be.' The other says: 'Christ has to be chosen, and always must be.' Though both are the truth, one is the truth as it is for God and as it is for faith the further side of decision; the other is the truth as it must be to the subject facing decision.

As far as the final issue of God's purpose is concerned, there can be only one outcome. All things must be summed up in Christ, because in principle all things already are. Hell is an ultimate impossibility, because *already* there *is* no one outside Christ. When the New Testament speaks from this point of view, this is its message. But to man in decision and to the preacher challenging man to decision, there remain two realities, not one. Here Jesus and the Apostles are equally unanimous that there *is* life and there *is* death. And they have no hesitation in saying that there are many, indeed most, who choose death.

And the death they choose is eternal death. That is to say, as they choose it and as long as they choose it, it is something that must present itself to them (or be made to present itself to them) as a choice which is final and irreversible. The believer, indeed, seeing the matter, as it were, from the other side of the divine act in Christ, knows that God cannot let it rest there; he must and will win all men. But what is fatal is to transfer this confidence, which is valid only for the subject ' in the truth,' to make it hold ' objectively ' apart from faith. To do so is to take the edge off all moral seriousness. A man comes to rely on something on which he has no right to rely—namely that ' God will put it all right in the end.' He says to himself, ' It does not matter now if I choose hell; for it is not finally fatal. Death is not really eternal after all. The alternative to life is not capital punishment as we had been told: it is reduced to life sentence— and, as everyone knows, life sentence does not really mean " for life ".' In this way the moral nerve is cut. What

is true in Christ has been turned into a damnable lie. The
reliance of faith on the utter mercy of God becomes the
blasphemous presumption of '*Dieu pardonnera: c'est son
métier.*'

It is not for nothing that the parable says that those on
the left hand went away into *eternal* punishment.[8] They had
chosen something which for them was of unlimited consequence. No man can reject Christ and claim a finite hell.
The man who sins, presuming grace will abound, self-assured
that God must see him through, can hear no word of grace.
His state is one where forgiveness is impossible. The Everlasting Mercy can come only to those who have wholly ceased
to take it for granted. The Word that speaks redemption can
come only as a 'nevertheless,' that is, to those who recognize
that, as far as they have power to evade it or right to reckon,
nothing can alter their state of eternal loss.

That is what the myth of the Sheep and the Goats asserts
by its uncompromising insistence on two endless spiritual
states. It upholds the eternal seriousness of the choice
before man. To choose hell, just as much as to choose
heaven, is to opt for something infinite: there can be no
rejection of eternity with limited liability. Nothing must
be allowed to weaken that seriousness—not even the truth
that in God all things must run out to a single issue. For
this, to the man in sin, is not a truth that can be taken into
account. As long as he thinks it can, as long as he presumes
upon it, it remains for him a lie: for there can come no

[8] The genuine universalist will base nothing on the fact (which
is a fact) that the New Testament word for eternal (*aionios*) does
not necessarily mean everlasting, but enduring only for an indefinitely
long period. For he can apply this signification to 'eternal punishment' in Matt. 25.46 only if he is willing to give exactly the
same sense to 'eternal life' in the same verse. As F. D. Maurice
said many years ago now, writing to F. J. A. Hort: 'I did not
see how *aionios* could mean one thing when it was joined with
kolasis and another when it was joined with *zoe*' (quoted, J. O. F.
Murray, *The Goodness and the Severity of God*, p. 195). To
admit that the two phrases are not parallel is at once to treat them
with unequal seriousness. And that a true universalism must
refuse to do.

'nevertheless' to the man who says, 'I told you so.' His state must be one of eternal hell—eternal, that is, as far as he is concerned as subject; it says nothing objectively of whether God's love cannot and will not turn even such a state as this to the faith that can make what is now a lie the truth for him.

Such, then, is the intention of the myth which depicts both heaven and hell as eternal states: it asserts both as realities, to the subject, of endless seriousness and unlimited consequence. The error comes when this picture is 'objectivized' as a description of the final condition of the universe as it is in God. The whole thing becomes transposed from the key of *kairos* into that of *chronos*. Infinite seriousness is translated as endless time: what is of eternal moment becomes what is of everlasting duration. And so we end with the familiar picture of heaven and hell as two objective realities finally and everlastingly co-existent side by side in God's universe. By such transposition the entire matter is turned from being the profoundest truth to the final lie. We are asked to believe that perpetually throughout eternity we must envisage the most terrible defeat of the love of God—the prospect, as it were, of the horrors of a concentration camp set in the midst of a blissful countryside.

But that cannot be, without negating all God is and denying all that in Christ he has done. With equal conviction as it declares the awfulness of the decision, the Gospel asserts that the final reality for the subject is *not* the final description of the universe in God. To all, as to each, the impossible, that on which no one can presume, must happen. Hell, so limitless to the man who has chosen it, is still bounded by the 'nevertheless' of divine love. And that love must win. 'Hereby shall we . . . assure our heart before him, *whereinsoever* our heart condemn us, because God is greater than our heart' (I John 3.19-20). The incredible must happen, because in Christ the incredible has happened. 'Our soul is escaped as a bird out of the snare of the fowler; the snare is broken and we are delivered' (Ps. 124.7). The world *has been* redeemed. Hell has been harrowed, and none

can finally make it their home. The shadow of the Cross
has fallen aslant it: the halls of death are condemned
property.

Let us conclude the matter with a parable. To man there
remain eternally two ways. And the one that is crowded is
still the one that leads to destruction; and many there be
that find it. But at some point on that road, be it far or near,
each one finds also something, or rather Someone, else. It
is a figure, stooping beneath the weight of a cross. 'Lord,
where are you going?' asks Everyman. And the answer comes:
'I am going to Rome, to Moscow, to New York, to be
crucified afresh in your place.' And no man in the end can
bear that encounter forever. For it is an encounter with
a power than which there can be nothing greater, a meeting
with omnipotent Love itself. This love will take no man's
choice from him; for it is precisely his choice that it wants.
But its will to lordship is inexhaustible and ultimately unendurable: the sinner *must* yield. God has exposed the
strong right arm by which he has declared that he will curb
the nations. And, lo, it is pierced by nails, stained with
blood, and riveted in impotence. Is it to us too an offence
and foolishness? Yet this is the authentic quality of love's
omnipotence. 'The weakness of God is stronger than men'
(1 Cor. 1.25)—than any man; for 'I, if I be lifted up from
the earth, will draw all men unto myself' (John 12.32).
Christ, in Origen's old words, remains on the Cross so long
as one sinner remains in hell. That is not speculation:
it is a statement grounded in the very necessity of God's nature.
In a universe of love there can be no heaven which tolerates
a chamber of horrors, no hell for any which does not at
the same time make it hell for God. He cannot endure
that, for *that* would be the final mockery of his nature. And
he will not.

CHAPTER XII

Conclusion

'There is a department in Christian theology which bears
the title "Eschatology" and deals with the "last things." It
claims to speak of the ultimate future of man and of certain
facts which are to occur "in the last times" or last in
time (a seemingly contradictory notion!) from which we are,
however, still happily far off and remote. Such an eschatology
represents no more than—in the apt phrase of Karl Barth
—innocent little chapters at the very end of Christian dogmatics far from any immediate concern for human life and
human consciousness. Few realize that, in point of fact,
*eschatology is not the teaching about the last things after
everything else but rather the teaching about the relation
of all things to the "last things" or, as it were, about the
lastness of all things.*'[1]
'The lastness of all things': that is a perspective uniquely
characteristic of the New Testament, having peculiar relevance
for an age such as ours. It does not imply a literal adventism
—whose message is of 'last things after everything else.'
It is not upheld by an expectation that the end of the world
will occur at any moment, nor is it fed by the illusion that
the sufferings of this generation must be uniquely those of the
Messianic tribulation. All these notions have indeed been
mixed up with it by perverse and wrong-headed people. In
particular, the possible destruction of everything in a nuclear
holocaust has produced its meed of apocalyptic; but this
merely proves the need of a sound theology to show how
'speculations about the end of the world derived from it are
not only scientifically implausible but religiously wrong.'[2]
The rediscovery of eschatology in our day has nothing to

[1] E. Lampert, *The Apocalypse of History*, p. 14. Italics mine.
[2] Reinhold Niebuhr, *Faith and History*, p. 269.

134

do with the apocalyptic nature of particular events, though it may have needed particular events to provoke it.

The recovered awareness is that 'the Christian lives not *at* the End of Time, but rather *from* the End and *in* the End of Time.'[3] He sees *everything* from an eschatological perspective. The Biblical world-view is not obtained by regarding all things under the form of a timeless eternity, nor as ideally they might be, but as they already are in Christ, the End. The Christian sees all history and all decisions *from the End*. And, from the End, the events of this present time and of every time can be given a new dimension through the forms of apocalyptic and the glass of vision. The effect of this glass is at first sight startling. The earth comes to be seen no longer as the battle-ground merely of flesh and blood, of ideologies and armies, of political forces and economic laws, of the Ego and the Id. Occupying the stage of history are descried great principalities and powers, world-rulers of this darkness locked in conflict with Michael and his angels, the spiritual hosts of the Messiah routing the legions of Satan and the Antichrist. These figures are wholly misunderstood if taken as denizens of another world than this. Rather, they are the kind of forms through which alone the true, eschatological depth of this world can adequately be portrayed. When the Seer set down his vision that ' there was war in heaven,' he meant it to describe not something going on in a separate, supernatural order above or behind our own, nor something merely that *will* take place one day—a ' last ' thing; he saw it, rather, as a description of *this* world, here and now and always, as it must appear when looked at *from the End*, ' in the Spirit, on the Day of the Lord.'

Christian eschatology is neither a tentative guess at how in distant ages the evolutionary process may work out; nor is it a specific programme of immediate catastrophe. It is the lighting up of a new dimension of life *now*. It introduces into the present a new astringency and a new urgency. ' Every instant of time becomes more momentous than ever—every instant is " eschatological," or, as one person has put it, like the point in the fairy-story where the clock is just about to strike twelve.'[4] And Max Warren gives this instance to show how the Bible forces men to view even the most commonplace in a new light: 'In 1 Pet. 2.11 the Christians are characterized by a word, *paroikoi*, which designated them by their legal status as non-citizens. Upon this word Dr. Selwyn has the following note—" The idea of Christians as sojourners in the world came to be felt as so expressive of their condition that *paroikia* became a common term for a Christian community in a place: hence our word parish." For Christians, even the most parochial affairs should be both strange and eschatological.'[5]

The fashion of this world looks different when seen from the End. The neutrality goes out of it. It is as though the beam of a searchlight has been turned upon it, immeasurably deepening the contrast between light and shade. The flatness is taken from living. A new edge and tone is given to it. The common round becomes charged with fresh moment and decisiveness.

It is precisely this gift that the modern world so desperately lacks. It is for this reason that it seeks outlet in man-made eschatologies. It is for this reason that it resorts to the artificial stimulants of gambling and drugs, and continually screws itself up to some new pitch of excitement and suspense. All these are attempts to re-create a lost sense of each moment as the day of decision, to restore the pinch of expectancy to a life which has become flat and dead and insipid.

But those who have breathed again the atmosphere of Christian eschatology, who in a tired and drab world have sniffed the clean, crisp air of the Advent message, have no need of such expedients. It is difficult to express in language the effect of this recovery. But there is perhaps an analogy which may convey a little of its feel. For there was a moment in recent English history when something of the transforming power of apocalypse was sensed as a shared

[4] H. Butterfield, *Christianity and History*, p. 121.
[5] *The Truth of Vision*, pp. 137-8.

experience of the nation. In the summer of 1940 we felt everything become braced to a sudden tautness. The slack went out of life. The indecision vanished. Blurred outlines leapt into focus. For a flash all stood out sharp and clear-cut, pin-pointed as in an etching. There was nothing artificial about this. The issues of life and death confronted us : there was no shuffling, no shrugging them off.

It is in such a 'moment' 'between the times' that the Christian life is set. It is of the very nature of Christian community to be an eschatological reality. This is a dimension to contemporary living which is I believe a distinctive contribution of the Christian Church. Of course, the Church, as well as tasting what the Epistle to the Hebrews calls 'the powers of the age to come' (6.5), has its life also very much in 'this age.' In so far as it is conformed to the latter, it wears the dull sub-lunary look with which none but its members are more familiar. But there is a spirit, what the New Testament calls *the* Spirit, that element of 'the last days' in the midst of these days, which is, in my experience, to be breathed here as nowhere else.

It is a spirit which, in these latter times, has been recovered for us largely through the churches of the persecution during and after the War. It is in such a setting that the relevance of apocalyptic—to a sane and ordered world so bizarre —always makes itself felt afresh. When this book was first being written, there was still something of that tingling, electrically charged atmosphere in which the myths of apocalyptic can take on an almost tangible reality. That was why it was important to let them stand forth *as myths*, to release them from fundamentalisms in which they had been encased and well-nigh killed. And I would not now wish to unsay any of that. For until we can see them as myths—and not as forecasts or fantasies—there is no possibility of their being reborn.

It is ironical nevertheless that, in contrast with the myths of the First Things, the myths of the End should have come to their own precisely as the demand to 'demythologize' became clamant. The spate of writing on 'the Christian

hope' in preparation for the 1954 Assembly of the World
Council of Churches coincided with the English translation
of *Kerygma and Myth*,[6] with its famous war-time essay by
Rudolf Bultmann propounding the urgent spiritual need to
strip down the New Testament proclamation and allow it to
step free of its mythological garb. The debate sparked
off by the latter quickly carried all before it, and deeper or
wider exploration of the Christian myth of the Last Things
was for the time being postponed.

All this coincided also with the relaxation of political
tension in Europe between East and West. Men drew back
from the edge, life began to return to normal, and apocalyptic
receded. A decade that was to be wooed by the slogan
'You've never had it so good' became increasingly disinter-
ested in brinkmanship, military or spiritual.

It is one of the ironies of eschatology that its relevance
is kept alive for most people only in cultural conditions
which create the apocalyptic that discredits it. This is a
process we have watched at work earlier in this book in
the history of the Old Testament, and in *Jesus and His
Coming* I have traced its operation in the New. Though the
apocalyptic atmosphere heightens the relevance, it also distorts
the perspective, of the prophetic message. And in this matter
I believe that Jesus and the earliest Christian preaching stand
spiritually with the prophets rather than the apocalyptists.
It is for this reason that they are able to speak to conditions
of relative tranquillity as well as to those of emergency and
stress.

For the time being at any rate most of us do not live
in an apocalyptic situation—though there are revolutionary
undercurrents in parts of our world, and indeed of our
lives, where the surface calm could quickly be shattered.
In this state of affairs, where hope must be translated
into terms of ongoing secularity rather than those of 'the
end of the age,' the need for an intelligent and valid
eschatology is, if anything, deeper. In the situation of Russia
in 1917 or Britain in 1940, hope, even against hope, is

[6] Vol. I, 1953.

comparatively easily formulated and sustained. There is an edge to living which gives it definition. In the greyer and gayer relativities of so-called peace-time existence, the slackness and the cynicism return. Hope becomes harder precisely as it becomes easier. To care and keep on caring, to struggle for justice when the glamour wears off, to continue being open to the next day and the next man, requires a more than usual, I would say a more than human, dimension in humanism. It is this dimension that in its origin inspired the Freedom Movement in the United States and kept it from going sour. Its haunting refrain 'We shall overcome some day' was profoundly influenced by the perspective of Biblical eschatology. Indeed its 'some day' is an almost exact equivalent of the prophets' use of 'that day' or 'that time'[7] to speak of their hope's horizon. For this the 'how long?' of *chronos* is not decisive. Yet it is no remote, far-off divine event at the end of time. It is a *kairos*, an hour, a day of the Lord, having an urgency and an imminence that brooks neither delay nor dissimulation.

What the Christian faith provides is not a blue-print for the future of man. Its hope is not set down on some divine scroll waiting to be unrolled. Its hope is in the Call, the Cry, implanted in nature and in history, which refuses to allow man finally to stop his ears. Its assurance rests in the fact that the whole of life is *response*, that the initiative—whether in the Beginning or the End—does not lie with us. It speaks of an evocation, a trust, an endurance, by which, in freedom, men find themselves impelled and drawn on. It points to those whose whole way of life betokens a 'beyond' that will not let them rest: 'For people who speak thus make it clear that they are seeking a homeland. If they had been thinking of that land from which they had gone out, they would have had opportunity to return' (Heb. 11.14-15: R.S.V.). But above all its pattern of life and hope and endurance is grounded in the overmastering constraint of a love which, once sensed, changes everything. 'For the love of Christ leaves us no choice,

[7] See John Marsh, *The Fulness of Time*, especially Chapter IV.

when once we have reached the conclusion that one man
died for all and therefore all mankind has died. His purpose
in dying for all was that men, while still in life, should
cease to live for themselves, and should live for him who
for their sake died and was raised to life. With us therefore worldly standards have ceased to count in our estimate
of any man; even if once they counted in our understanding
of Christ, they do so now no longer. When anyone is
united to Christ, there is a new world; the old order has
gone, and a new order has already begun ' (2 Cor. 5.14-17:
N.E.B.). Such is the distinctively Christian perspective and
outlook on life.

Bibliography

P. Althaus, *Die letzten Dinge,* fourth edition, Gütersloh, 1933.

Thomas J. J. Altizer, *The Gospel of Christian Atheism,* London, Collins, 1967; Philadelphia, Westminster Press, 1966.

(with W. Hamilton) *Radical Theology and the Death of God,* Indianapolis, Bobbs-Merrill, 1966.

John Baillie, *And the Life Everlasting,* London, Oxford University Press, 1934; New York, Scribner's, 1933.

James Barr, *Biblical Words for Time,* London, SCM Press, 1962.

H. W. Bartsch, *Kerygma and Myth,* London, S.P.C.K., Volume I, 1953; New York, Harper's Torchbook, 1961.

Dietrich Bonhoeffer, *Letters and Papers from Prison,* first published in English, London SCM Press, 1953 (third revised edition, 1967), Fontana, 1959; as *Prisoner for God,* New York, Macmillan Co., 1959.

Kenneth Boulding, *The Meaning of the 20th Century: The Great Transition,* London, Allen & Unwin, 1965; New York, Harper & Row, 1964.

E. Brunner, *The Mediator,* first published in English, London, Lutterworth Press, 1934; Philadelphia, Westminster Press, 1947.

The Christian Doctrine of God, first published in English, London, Lutterworth Press, 1949; Philadelphia, Westminster Press, 1950.

141

Eternal Hope, first published in English, London, Lutterworth Press, 1954; Philadelphia, Westminster Press, 1954.

Truth as Encounter, first published in English, London, SCM Press, 1964 (formerly as *The Divine-Human Encounter,* 1943); Philadelphia, Westminster Press, 1964.

Herbert Butterfield, *Christianity and History,* London, G. Bell & Sons, 1949, Fontana, 1957; New York, Scribner's, 1950.

Ed. D. Callahan, *The Secular City Debate,* New York, Macmillan Co., 1966, distributed in Europe by Collier-Macmillan.

Pierre Teilhard de Chardin, *The Phenomenon of Man,* first published in English, London, Collins, 1959; New York, Harper & Row, 1959, revised edition and Fontana, 1965.

Le Milieu Divin, first published in English, London, Collins, 1960, Fontana, 1964; *The Divine Milieu,* New York, Harper & Row, 1960.

The Future of Man, first published in English, London, Collins, 1964; New York, Harper & Row, 1964.

Hymn of the Universe, first published in English, London, Collins, 1965; New York, Harper & Row, 1965.

R. H. Charles, *A Critical history of the doctrine of a future life in Israel, in Judaism, and in Christianity,* London, A. & C. Black, 1899; second revised edition, 1913.

Immortality, Drew Lecture, London, Oxford University Press, 1912.

H. G. Cox, *The Secular City,* London, SCM Press, 1965; New York, Macmillan Co., 1965.

Oscar Cullmann, *Christ and Time,* first published in English, London, SCM Press, 1951, revised edition 1962; Philadelphia, Westminster Press, revised edition 1964.

L. Dewart, *The Future of Belief, London*, Burns & Oates, 1967; New York, Herder & Herder, 1966.

C. H. Dodd, *The Parables of the Kingdom*, Welwyn, James Nisbet, 1935, revised edition 1961, London, Fontana, 1961; New York, Scribner's, 1935, revised edition 1961.

Lloyd Douglas, *The Robe*, London, Peter Davies, 1943; Boston, Houghton Mifflin Co., 1942.

T. S. Eliot, 'Ash Wednesday', 'The Dry Salvages' in *Collected Poems 1909-62*, London, Faber & Faber, 1963; New York, Harcourt, Brace & World Inc., 1963.

J. E. Fison, *The Christian Hope*, London, Longmans Green, 1954.

J. G. Frazer, *The Golden Bough*, London, Macmillan & Co., 1890, St. Martin's Library, 1962; New York, Macmillan Co., 1960.

Dom Bede Frost, *Modern Substitutes for Christianity*, Oxford, A. R. Mowbray, 1942; New York, Morehouse-Barlow Co. Inc., 1942.

R. Garaudy, *From Anathema to Dialogue*, London, Collins, 1967; New York, Herder & Herder, 1966.

Ed. H. L. Goudge, *II Corinthians*, London, Methuen, 1943.

William Hamilton, (with Thomas J. J. Altizer), *Radical Theology and the Death of God*, Indianapolis, Bobbs-Merrill, 1966.

F. C. Happold, *Religious Faith and Twentieth Century Man*, London, Pelican, 1966; New York, Penguin Inc., 1966. *The Interpreter's Dictionary of the Bible*, Vol. 4, Nashville, Tennessee, Abingdon Press, 1962, distributed in England by Nelson's, 1963.

W. James, 'The Dilemma of Determinism', first published 1884, reprinted in ed. A. Castell, *Essays in Pragmatism*, New York, Hafner Co., 1948.

Nikos Kazantzakis, *Report to Greco*, first published in English, Oxford, Bruno Cassirer, distributed by Faber & Faber, 1965; New York, Simon & Schuster, 1966.

S. Kierkegaard, *Concluding Unscientific Postscript*, first published in English, London, Oxford University Press, 1942; Princeton University Press, 1941.

K. E. Kirk, *The Vision of God*, London, Longmans Green, 1934.

H. Knight, *The Hebrew Prophetic Consciousness*, London, Lutterworth Press, 1948.

E. Lampert, *The Apocalypse of History*, London, Faber & Faber, 1948.

Ed. D. M. Mackinnon, *Christian Faith and Communist Faith*, London, Macmillan & Co., 1953.

H. R. Mackintosh, *Immortality and the Future*, London, Hodder & Stoughton, 1915.

J. Maritain, *True Humanism*, first published in English, London, G. Bles, 1938.

John Marsh, *The Fulness of Time*, Welwyn, James Nisbet, 1952.

Ed. W. R. Miller, *The New Christianity*, New York, Delacorte Press, 1967.

P. S. Minear, *Christian Hope and the Second Coming*. Philadelphia, Westminster Press, 1954.

James Moffatt, *The Thrill of Tradition*, London, SCM Press, 1944; New York, Macmillan Co., 1944.

J. Moltmann, *Theology of Hope*, first published in English, London, SCM Press, 1967.

C. F. D. Moule, *The Meaning of Hope*, London, Highway Press, 1953.

J. O. F. Murray, *The Goodness and the Severity of God*, London, SCM Press, 1924.

Reinhold Niebuhr, *Faith and History*, Welwyn, James Nisbet, 1949; New York, Scribner's, 1949.

Thomas W. Ogletree, *The 'Death of God' Controversy*, London, SCM Press, 1966; Nashville, Tennessee, Abingdon Press, 1966.

O. C. Quick, *Doctrines of the Creed*, Welwyn, James Nisbet, 1938, London, Fontana, 1963; New York, Scribner's, 1938.

The Gospel of the New World, Welwyn, James Nisbet, 1944.

Alan Richardson, *Christian Apologetics*, London, SCM Press, 1947; New York, Harper & Row, 1947.

J. A. T. Robinson, *The Body*, London, SCM Press, 1952; distributed in U.S.A. by Alec R. Allenson.

Jesus and His Coming, London, SCM Press, 1957; Nashville, Tennessee, Abingdon Press, 1957.

Christ Comes In, Oxford, A. R. Mowbray, 1960.

On Being the Church in the World, London, SCM Press, 1960; Philadelphia, Westminster Press, 1962.

Honest to God, London, SCM Press, 1963; Philadelphia, Westminster Press, 1963.

Exploration into God, London, SCM Press, 1967; Stanford University Press, 1967.

A. Schweitzer, *The Mysticism of Paul the Apostle*, London, A. & C. Black, 1931; New York, Macmillan Co., 1955.

E. G. Selwyn, *I Peter*, London, Macmillan & Co., 1946.

Ronald Gregor Smith, *Secular Christianity,* London, Collins, 1966; New York, Harper & Row, 1966.

Paul Tillich, *The Shaking of the Foundations,* London, SCM Press, 1949, Pelican, 1962; New York, Scribner's, 1948.

A. R. Vidler, *Christ's Strange Work,* London, Longmans Green, 1944, and by SCM Press, 1963.

Max Warren, *The Truth of Vision,* London, Canterbury Press, 1948.

Leslie Weatherhead, *The Christian Agnostic,* London, Hodder & Stoughton, 1965; Nashville, Tennessee, Abingdon Press, 1965.

John & Charles Wesley, *A Selection of Hymns on the Lord's Supper,* Southport, Methodist Sacramental Fellowship, 1936.

Colin Williams, *Faith in a Secular Age,* London, Fontana, 1966; New York, Harper & Row, 1966.

Index

147